TRUST IN MIND

TRUST IN MIND

The Rebellion of Chinese Zen

Mu Soeng

foreword by Jan Chozen Bays

WISDOM PUBLICATIONS • BOSTON

Wisdom Publications
199 Elm Street
Somerville MA 02144 USA
www.wisdompubs.org

Library of Congress Cataloging-in-Publication Data available
Mu, Soeng.
Trust in mind : the rebellion of Chinese Zen / Mu Soeng; foreword by Jan Chozen Bays.
p. cm.
Includes bibliographical references and index.
ISBN 0-86171-391-5 (pbk. : alk. paper) -- ISBN 0-86171-391-5
1. Sengcan, d. 606 Xin xin ming. 2. Spiritual life—Zen Buddhism.
I. Title.
BQ9288.M84 2004
294.3'85—dc22
                                        2004000199

Cover design by Rick Snizik. Interior design by Gopa&Ted2. Set in Renard 3, 8/10

Blyth, R. H. "The Believing Mind" is reprinted from *Zen and Zen Classics,*
Volume One, published by The Hokuseido Press, Tokyo, 1960.

"A Song of Enlightenment" translated by Philip Dunn and Peter Jourdan is reprinted from
The Book of Nothing, published by Andrews McMeel Publishing, Kansas City, MO, 2002.
© The Book Laboratory Inc. California.

"Trust in Mind." Private translation by Stanley Lombardo is reprinted
with permission from the translator.

"Have Faith in Your Mind" translated by Lu Kuan Yu (Charles Luk) is reprinted
from *Practical Buddhism,* published by Rider & Co. Ltd., London, 1971.

"Faith in Mind" translated by Master Sheng-yen is reprinted from *The Poetry of Enlightenment:
Poems by Ancient Chan Masters.* Elmhurst, NY: Dharma Drum Publications, 1987.

"Inscribed on the Believing Mind" translated by D.T. Suzuki is reprinted from
Essays in Zen Buddhism, First Series. York Beach, Maine: Samuel Weiser, Inc., 1949.

Waley, Arthur (ed.) "On Trust in the Heart" is reprinted from
Buddhist Texts Through the Ages. New York: Harper & Row, 1964.

Wisdom Publications' books are printed on acid-free paper and meet the guidelines for permanence and durability of the Committee on Production Guidelines for Book Longevity of the Council on Library Resources.

Printed in the United States of America

∝≪ Table of Contents ≫∝

❧ Foreword ❦

THIS BOOK BY Mu Soeng is a welcome one, as there are only a few resources or commentaries on the "Trust in Mind" poem available currently in English. Mu Soeng combines what he calls "library understanding" and "zendo understanding" in a manner accessible to both those who study Zen or Chan in books and those who study Zen on the meditation cushion. The early founders of Japanese Zen temples and centers in America (Roshis Suzuki, Katagiri, Maezumi, and Kapleau) emphasized direct inquiry into the nature of Mind through meditation and silent retreats and not through academic study. Perhaps some of them knew that their time with us was short, and they winnowed their task down to the essential: helping us touch the mind of the Buddha, experience the deeply quiet mind, and encounter the flashes of direct knowing that arise from it. Our minds were chock full of odd ideas about meditation and enlightenment and our teachers had only a little time to entice us into dropping those notions and doing the hard work that would enable us to taste the actual experience of the bright clarity of samadhi and the deep flow of prajna wisdom.

In the introduction to this book Mu Soeng first pulls back from the sutra to help us understand the historical and philosophical environment that shaped the life and beliefs of the Buddhist ancestor who composed this song of enlightenment. Although the third Zen ancestor Sengcan may not have been the actual author, it was some Zen ancestor who gave us this poem which has endured to instruct and inspire Zen students for 1,300 years. Ancestors are those who leave descendants, and we who read, study, and chant this sutra are the descendants of the enlightened master who sang this most happy song.

As we look at the past we think that things were fixed, that Chan Buddhism arose fully formed as its own distinct entity. Mu Soeng points

out that as Buddhism enters new countries and cultures it subtly incorpo-
rates and adapts preexisting beliefs and practices. *Trust in Mind* is a cre-
ation arising from the blending of Indian Buddhist, Chinese Taoist, and
Chinese Chan doctrine. A similar mingling of religious streams is occur-
ring at this time in America: witness the earnest practitioners and groups
who self-identify as, for example, Catholic-Zen, Quaker-Vipassana, or
Judeo-Buddhist. Because we are in the midst of this cross fertilization
process, we cannot perceive it with the objectivity of a historian. Perhaps
an enlightenment poem that will last for millennia will arise in modern
times. May it be so.

At Great Vow Zen Monastery, we chant Sengcan's poem every day dur-
ing our weeklong meditation retreats and it is a favorite among many peo-
ple because it gives such clear instructions on how to proceed toward
liberation from the tyranny of mind. In many different ways the poem
makes one essential point: don't let the mind fall into comparisons—at all!
It abjures us with a listing, line by line, of the many opposites that we
should not let arise in the mind. Thirty-four pairs of opposites are used as
examples of what not to think about: love and hate, like and dislike, heaven
and earth, for and against, lack and excess, accepting and rejecting, outer
things and inner feelings, activity and passivity, one and the other, assertion
and denial, emptiness and reality, this and that, right and wrong, dualities
and One, object and subject, coarse and fine, easy and difficult, fast and slow,
coming and going, free and in bondage, dislike and accept, wise and fool-
ish, one and many, rest and unrest, illusion and enlightenment, gain and
loss, right and wrong, stationary and moving, movement and rest, self and
other-than-self, large and small, Being and non-Being, one thing and all
things, yesterday and tomorrow.

If you let go of all these opposites your mind might become very quiet and
very expansive, resting in a state of radical inclusion. All spiritual work is
aimed at developing our highest human potential, to live in a complex and
often violent world with a mind that can be trusted to be clear and wise, and
a heart that is undefended and open to all beings. The key to unlocking this
potential lies in being able to cease our habit of sorting and judging. All great
spiritual teachers have given us the same message and it reminds us of our
primary purpose in undertaking a life of religious practice. We must open
the gateway, not just to our full potential as human beings, but ultimately to
freedom from the suffering that seems inherent in a human life.

Dogen Zenji, the great Zen master of the thirteenth century, advised, "Simply think of non-thinking." With this, Dogen invites us to fill the mind with something other than thinking—with, for example, mantra, or the simple question of a koan, or best of all, pure awareness. Dogen also wrote that the mind of enlightenment is a mind that is aware of impermanence, of discontinuity, of ceaseless birth and death. This does not mean that the enlightened mind thinks about impermanence, but rather that it has a continuous experience of the actual functioning in this moment of impermanence, of arising and disappearing.

In the Pali canon, the Buddha recounts that as he sat under the Bodhi tree, just on the brink of enlightenment, he reached a stage where his mind was purified, bright, unblemished, light, and rid of imperfection. What is this imperfection of which he was rid? It is simply self-centered thought. When we examine discursive thoughts, all comparing and judging thoughts, we discover they are all self-centered. Even self-critical thoughts are self-centered; high self-esteem and low self-esteem are both forms of esteeming the self. If we are to experience for ourselves the Truth that we earnestly long for, we must find a way to suspend, for a time, the thought-function of the mind and activate the awareness-function. Only when we enter pure awareness do subject and object drop away and we leave behind the confusion and anxiety of the realm of individual mind to enter the eternal serenity of the realm of One Mind.

We have relied upon this individual and self-referring mind since our early childhood, when we began to speak and thus to think, when we became self-aware and thus other-aware. In relying on this mind we were finding safety and comfort in the same mind that mankind has relied upon since speech first arose hundreds of thousands of years ago. To step out of the ceaseless activity of this mind we have to take the "backward step" of meditation—to return to a preverbal and even prehuman awareness of the sounds, touches, colors, tastes, and smells of reality-as-it-is. This is not easy, but when it occurs, it plunges us into a most natural and flowing life, unrestricted by human bonds, like a bird dancing in air, a fish flying in water, a tree swimming in the wind, or a still pebble amid a dust storm. So what does it mean to live with complete trust in Mind? As Mu Soeng aptly points out, although the One Mind does not change, the meaning of Trust in Mind can change according to the cultural context. In Buddhist India it might mean trust in the mind's ability to be trained, to be cleared of delusion, and thus to reach a nonverbal, nonconceptual spaciousness, permeated by happiness and equanimity, a state from which insights easily arise. In Taoist China it might mean trust in the Way, in a natural and spontaneous functioning that intuitively aligns with the wisdom of natural forces and wastes no energy by going against them. In early Chan it might mean cultivation of nondual mind, or nonaction and nonthought. This leads to perception without clinging, (*tathata* or suchness), to cognition without clinging (*shunyata* or emptiness) and to functioning without clinging (*upaya* or skillful means). Once this becomes one's "normal" way of functionimg, mind-to-mind transmission of the Dharma has occurred.

Our personal experience of Trust in Mind also changes as meditation practice changes us. Early in our practice-life, trust means belief that there is indeed a way to end needless suffering. We dare to hope that if we undertake the path laid out by the buddhas and ancestors, we too can become not just less burdened but truly free. We could come into our full birthright of mind and heart. We can develop the qualities of clarity, penetrating insight, flexibility and breadth, compassion, joy and equanimity. As our practice matures, blind faith is replaced by lived experience. We begin to taste for ourselves the fruit harvested from cultivation of the heart/mind, and confidence arises. This is the second aspect of Trust in Mind, trust in the Mind of the Buddhas and ancestors and the willingness to follow their instructions.

As we experience the emergence of our own Buddha mind and watch it at work in the world we marvel at its mysterious and mathematically appropriate functioning. This is the third aspect of Trust in Mind.

Gradually we relinquish our old habit patterns. Less and less do we fall back on strategies developed by the small self-centered and self-referential mind in reaction to life's inevitable buffeting and wounds. Renouncing the ways of the small and fearful mind and allow the one Mind/Heart to begin to carry us and to function through our bodies and minds is the fourth aspect of Trust in Mind.

Finally our old structure of body and mind fall away and we are turned inside out to an "outside" that is immeasurably vast. Then we function in a realm devoid of the usual landmarks of past and future, them and me. Traveling through a flowing landscape of beings and events, we greet everything with a serene interest and a happiness born of the experience of being always at home.

Chant Sengcan's poem day by day, year after year, and eventually its wisdom will work its way deep into the subconscious. There it lies, awaiting the right circumstances. Then, in an unexpected instant an event in our life meets the poem exactly, and the song of awakening suddenly becomes our own celebration of joyful understanding and liberation. And in this way we begin to live a life of Trust in Mind. We cease fearing the fundamental truths of life—impermanence, suffering, and the emptiness of self—and are able to release our minds and bodies into their flow. Then we discover that, precisely because they are always true, they are a source of refuge. The things that we need to accomplish our awakening are brought to us, and over time, faith grows to complete trust.

All is well, all manner of things are well.

Jan Chozen Bays

Jan Chozen Bays is the co-abbott of Great Vow Zen Monastery and the author of *Jizo Bodhisattva: Guardian of Children, Travelers, and other Voyagers.*

❧ Preface ❧

THE POEM *Hsin Shin Ming (Xinxinming)*, here translated as *Trust in Mind*, is one of the most beloved texts of the Zen tradition and one of the most familiar of the early Zen texts. Its first line, "The Great Way is not difficult for those who have no preferences" is celebrated in Chinese literature in much the same way as the first line of *Tao Te Ching*: "The Tao is that which cannot be talked about; that which can be talked about is not the Tao." Even today *Trust in Mind* continues to inspire countless admirers with its intimations, intuitively perceived, of the nature of a life lived in freedom. Attributed to Seng-ts'an (Jianzhi Sengcan; d. 606), the third ancestor of Chan (as Zen was known in China, and alternatively rendered *Ch'an*) in medieval China, this poem is a historically valuable document, an exploration of which gives us a glimpse into the genesis of a new movement that was to transform Chinese Buddhism. Now identified by historians as "Buddho-Taoism," this movement found its fullest flowering in Chan (itself a transliteration of the Sanskrit word *dhyana*, and later transliterated into Japanese as *Zen* and Korean as *Son*. I have used the term *Chan* throughout this commentary rather than the more familiar *Zen* since it has a distinct flavor of its own, and contrasts at times greatly with the historical Zen of Japan). Chan was to revolutionize both the understanding and application of Buddhist teachings in China, and it is this revolutionized version that became a favorite of poets and artists in the West in the 1950s and 1960s.

Now that a generation has matured and we have become more familiar with a wider range of Buddhist teachings, it seems appropriate that we continue to excavate the Indian and Chinese roots of Zen and Buddhism. The purpose of this commentary is to consider the historical and textual layers behind the theme of "One Mind" in Sengcan's poem because such consideration breaks open the core issue of awakening/realization that's central not only to Chan but the entire Buddhist tradition. We'll examine not only in what prior textual materials and traditions Sengcan might have drawn upon but also how his theme continues to resonate for subsequent generations both in Chan Buddhism and non-Chan Buddhist traditions. What does the poem tell us about Sengcan's purposes? Is it a "Song of Realization" of a saint, or is it meant to be a teaching device? Perhaps both? The two genres are easily reconciled in Chan and the *siddha* tradition of Vajrayana Buddhism where it is assumed that this type verse or song is expressing the moment of realization or awakening and that in so doing it can offer "pointing words" for others to themselves awaken.

In addition to throwing light on how Buddhist teachings were reconfigured in early medieval China, I hope also to provide a glimpse of a parallel reconfiguration taking place in contemporary America. The preceding several decades have brought under the single roof of America an unprecedented availability of Buddhist teachings from all traditions, and we are just now beginning the task of sorting out the various contexts of these teachings and their applicability for our own time and place. A proper contextualization of the Indian and Chinese backgrounds of this reconfiguration, besides enriching our own understanding, may have the value of evaluating these teachings as something more than a passing fad.

The reader should bear in mind that scholars (D. T. Suzuki and Shengyen, among others) question both the dating and authorship of the poem. Within the context of early Zen history, this is a generic rather than a specific problem. Sengcan's poem represents a certain genre that might collectively be called "the poetry of enlightenment." We might even see this genre as a continuation of an old tradition from India to China: the awakening poems by the monks and nuns (collected in *Theragatha* and *Therigatha*, respectively, of the Pali Canon) of the Buddha's time. In China, a number of texts within this genre are attributed to authors about whom we have little reliable biographical information. It may be that the power of this genre has to do with the content rather than who the author might have been. It may also be that the final form of the poem attributed to Sengcan is a composite, parts of which may have been composed by Sengcan himself but improved upon in later generations. Some of the language and thoughts in the poem may even belong to mid-Tang in China, some two centuries later. But it's hard to make the case, I think, that the attribution of the poem to Sengcan is totally fictitious. In a broader picture, a number of building blocks in early

Zen history are suspect, including the biographical details of Bodhidharma and Huineng, the founder and the sixth ancestor of Chinese Zen, respectively. In each case there is some germane detail that has been embellished upon for reasons that remain opaque to us.

In this commentary I take the position that within the genre of the poetry or songs of enlightenment what really matters is the perspective and investigation of deep truth rather than any hard-edged claim about the authorship. Even when I mention Sengcan by name, I have in mind the voice and face of a multitude of generations of Zen practitioners for whom a consideration of the deep truth was literally a matter of life and death. Sengcan must thus be considered a symbolic rather than a literal figure.

This commentary locates itself in my own training in the Sino-Korean Zen tradition. The thoughts and reflections shared here have been shaped as well by number of courses I have taught on Mahayana, Zen, and (Xinxinming) itself over the years. These teaching situations have provided me with a venue for greater understanding, and a greater appreciation for the nuances embedded in the text under consideration here.

Several friends were kind enough to read the first draft while this book was still a work in progress. I have benefited greatly from suggestions by Ven. Thanissaro Bhikkhu, Stephen Cope, Rajesh Kasturirangan, Greg Kramer, Linda Paul, and Courtney Schlosser. I thank them all for the generosity of their time and care. I hope they are forgiving of my stubbornness when I have not accepted their suggested changes. My stubbornness also allows me to take complete responsibility for any errors of interpretation or presentation that might fill the pages of this book. Thanks are due also to Larry Rosenberg for his quiet support and gentle encouragement throughout the writing of this book. Stanley Lombardo was generous in sharing his translation of Sengcan's poem and perspectives on its poetic structure. This book owes much of its final shape to the generous help I received from Josh Bartok, my editor at Wisdom Publications. His background in Zen practice was a perfect fit in fine-tuning the perspectives offered here.

I am thankful, as well, to Sensei Jan Chozen Bays for her kindness in writing the foreword for this commentary. Her extensive training in Zen tradition offers the reader certain insights that I may not have been able to clarify myself.

Finally, Barre Center for Buddhist Studies has been my home for many years now and it continues to provide inspiration and environment for intellectual and meditative explorations. Thanks to all my colleagues there for their support.

✒ A Note on the Pronunciation ✑ of Chinese Names

THE TRANSLITERATION SYSTEM used in this book for Chinese names is primarily Pinyin, with the Wade-Giles equivalent given in parenthesis after the first occurrence.

It should be noted that the third ancestor's name, transliterated as *Sengcan* in Pinyin, is pronounced akin to "sungtsan" and the name of the poem whose title is translated *Trust in Mind* and transliterated *Xinxinming* is pronounced akin to sibilant "Shinshinming."

PINYIN PRONUNCIATION

Vowels

a is pronounced "ah" as in the English word *swat*.

e is pronounced "uh" similar to the English word *fun*, or the familiar Chinese phrase *feng shui* ("fung shuay").

i alone or after a single (non-compound) consonant other than is pronounced "ee" as in the English word *magazine* (although the syllable *ri* is roughly pronounced "er" as in the English word *batter*).

i after *ch*, *sh*, or *zh* is a neutral vowel like "uh" almost nonexistent, plus *-r*, somewhat akin to the English word *shirk*.

o is pronounced "oh" as in the English word *note*.

u is pronounced "ü" like the French word *tu* or German word *über*.

Diphthongs

ao is pronounced "ow" as in the name Chairman Mao, and similar to the English word how.

ou is pronounced "oh" as in the English word *soul*.

ui is pronounced "uay" similar to the English word *way* or the familiar Chinese phrase *feng shui* ("fung shuay").

Consonants

c is pronounced "ts" similar to the English word *bats*.

q is pronounced "ch" similar to the English word *cheese* or the familiar martial art *qi gong*.

x is pronounced somewhere between the English letters *s* and *sh*.

zh is pronounced similar to the English letter *j*.

Pronunciations of most other consonants and consonant combinations are similar to English.

⋙ Introduction ⋘

CHAN WAS BORN out of what might be described as a nuanced sensibility of the absurdity of the human condition. This was the gift of Zhuangzi (alternatively Chuang Tzu) to Indian Buddhism in China. Indian Buddhism in India could at times be almost grim and somewhat puritanical, unable to laugh at its own predicaments of bondage and attempts at liberation. This, to a large extent, had to do with Buddhism having to be embedded within the larger religious culture of Brahmanism where religion was a source of power and authority. While no less serious about the enterprise of liberation, Chan found a tool-kit in the deconstruction of language rather than an entanglement with linguistic concepts and categories of ontology and counter-ontology. For that Chan is eternally indebted to Zhuangzi and other Taoist philosophers who, in the centuries before, had played with language in a creative and deconstructive manner. The spirit of Chan was kept alive through centuries by poets of the nondual. Sengcan, in the sixth century, was one such poet.

Chan is often viewed as a wholly indigenous Chinese Buddhist movement with no Indian counterpart. Indeed, Hu Shih, the noted scholar of modern China, started a simmering controversy when he asserted that Chan/Zen "was nothing short of a Chinese revolt against Buddhism."[1] His assertions came (in 1932) in response to the position taken by D. T. Suzuki who had introduced Zen Buddhism to the West with his seminal *Essays in Zen Buddhism, First Series* (1927), and who had firmly placed Chan/Zen within the context of Indian Buddhism.

Indeed there are contemporary scholars who follow Hu's line of thinking and declare,

Zen is Taoism disguised as Buddhism. When twelve hundred years of Buddhist accretions are removed from Zen, it is revealed to be a direct evolution of the spirit and philosophy of Taoism. Indeed, the literature known as the Laozi and Zhuangzi begins a continuous tradition that can be followed through the Chan of China to the Zen of present-day Japan. The formative writings of early Taoism are essentially the teachings of Zen.[2]

This commentary on *Trust in Mind* (my preferred translation of *Xinxinming*) is sympathetic to Suzuki's position even while acknowledging that perhaps the "spirit" of Chan can be seen as something distinct from the later institutionalized forms of Chan and Zen Buddhism. The institutional development of Buddhism in China is a collaborative effort between Chinese rulers and monks from Central Asia and native Chinese monks. It is a product, for the most part, of a certain type of State Buddhism that really has no counterpart in Indian Buddhism. A proper correlation, within the context of *Trust in Mind*, is the spirit of Chan and the spirit of the Buddha.

Trust in Mind is one of the first in a series of persuasive arguments to allow us to make a tenuous separation between the spirit of Chan and Chan Buddhism—by which I mean the later institutionalized Chan of Sung China and later centuries (roughly eleventh century onward). But to insist that early Chan had nothing to do with Indian Buddhism seems an unnecessarily harsh and indefensible position. Almost all contemporary scholars of Chan make allowance for its Indian roots even as they have found contradictions and inflations in Chan's self-claims for its history. Sheng-yen, one of the most respected Asian teachers of Chan in the West in modern times, has written extensively on *Trust in Mind* and other poems of "enlightenment" by Chan practitioners. His position is that these

Poets were not only highly accomplished practitioners, they were also well-versed in literature, history and Buddhist scholarship. In these poems we can discern references to Chinese philosophical, religious and literary history as well as to the roots and theories of Indian Buddhism.[3]

It is the position of this commentary that even though the language and sentiments expressed here have a Taoist flavor without the use of Pali or

Sanskrit words, these teachings are, by and large, a reworking of the Madhya-mika dialectic of Nagarjuna. (Of course, there are scholars who contend that Nagarjuna, the legendary founder of the Madhyamika school of Indian Mahayana, was not a Buddhist at all, or that Madhyamika dialectic is not Buddhist—but that's a different book!)

The intention of this commentary is to highlight an organic link between the sentiments of *Trust in Mind* and the core ideas of Mahayana Buddhism, and Madhyamika. Heinrich Dumoulin, the eminent historian of Zen, has written,

> There has been a tendency to find Zen so radically different from other Buddhist schools, especially during the Zen boom in America, that a distinction was drawn between Zen and Buddhism in general. It goes without saying that this sort of distinction is nonsense. Zen in its entirety belongs to Chinese Mahayana Buddhism.[4]

The attempt in this commentary, then, is to understand a sixth-century Chinese Buddhist text whose language is Taoist but whose teachings are very much Buddhist; to situate it in the tradition of Buddho-Taoism, and in the process get a sense of both Buddhist and Taoist ideas, and how they influenced each other to produce Chan or Zen. In doing so, it is always useful to keep in mind the injunction of Edward Conze, the premier historian of Prajnaparamita literature in the second half of the twentieth century

> Throughout its history, Buddhism has the unity of an organism, in that each new development takes place in continuity from the previous one. Nothing could look more different from a tadpole than a frog and yet they are stages of the same animal, and evolve continuously from each other. The Buddhist capacity for meta-morphosis must astound those who only see the end-products separated by long intervals of time, as different as chrysalis and butterfly. In fact they are connected by many gradations, which lead from one to the other and which only close study can detect. There is in Buddhism really no innovation, but what seems so is in fact a subtle adaptation of pre-existing ideas. Great attention has always been paid to continuous doctrinal development and to the proper transmission of the teaching. These are not the

anarchic philosophizing of individualists who strive for original-
ity at all costs.[5]

Of course, as Chan tradition was to insist, there can be no true under-
standing of Chan's use of Madhyamika dialectic outside the experiential
Chan. The role of practice is preeminent in Chan tradition; everything must
be submitted to an "uncorrupted" or "direct" personal experience that is
available before the consciousness is overwhelmed by linguistic formula-
tions and begins to engender self-deception. *Trust in Mind* speaks eloquently
to this layer of personal experience and this commentary seeks to reinforce
that approach.

My reading of Buddhist history is that the Buddha (whether we consider
him a religious or philosophical thinker) represents a revolution of thought
in his own time and place. Chan, in its methodology, is equally revolution-
ary in medieval China, quite unlike anything that has gone before in the evo-
lution of Buddhist culture and sensibility. It is as if each poet of Chan
consciously ignored centuries of codification of Buddha's teachings both in
China and India and connected directly with the Buddha's mind—especially
the mind with which he sat under the bodhi tree before his awakening expe-
rience. The "Chan rebellion" sought to connect itself with the liberating
spirit of the Buddha. The self-perception of Chan was that it was rearticu-
lating the deep experiential insights of the Buddha himself. Thus while
intending to contextualize this underlying pedigree of *Trust in Mind*, this
commentary is also mindful of Thomas Merton's observation that,

> Zen is not theology and it makes no claim to deal with theologi-
> cal truth in any form whatsoever. Nor is it an abstract metaphysics.
> It is, so to speak, a concrete and lived ontology which explains
> itself not in theoretical propositions but in acts emerging out of
> a certain quality of consciousness and of awareness. Only by these
> acts and by this quality of consciousness can Zen be judged. The
> paradoxes and seemingly absurd propositions it makes have no
> point except in relation to an awareness that is unspoken and
> unspeakable.[6]

This commentary is written out of the conviction that the basic teachings
of the Buddha are as relevant to us today as they were in Buddha's own

time, and that the admonitions made in *Xinxinming* speak eloquently to those teachings and affirm them for us much as they did for people in medieval China.

While the poem belongs chronologically to a simpler, pre-modern world, its sentiments speak clearly to one basic human longing: a wish to be at ease in the world. (A Buddhist from the Theravada tradition might argue that this sense of ease is directed more toward a trans-life perspective, but that argument does not necessarily preclude the wish to be at ease in this life.) This wish to be at ease may be felt much more deeply as a longing to completeness. Buddha's teachings offer *nirvana* as a synonym for completeness, a closure on the working of *dukkha*, the sense of incompleteness, in our lives. Sengcan's poem provides a highly nuanced understanding of Buddha's nirvana and in its contexts provides us with a template for life without grasping. Today we live distressed and fragmented lives in a complex world, but our wish to be at ease with ourselves and with the world around us, to be complete, is no different in its longing than that of all the generations who have gone before us. Perhaps our need for that ease is even greater today with all the stresses brought about by our membership in a technologized society that lives at hyperspeed.

A parallel understanding of being at ease comes from the biological sciences where researchers have seen that animals, dominated wholly by the "ancient" or limbic brain, are always alert to the potential danger all around them, yet within this alertness there is an ease of being which together we might call "tranquil and alert." Since the humans are inheritors of the limbic brain as well, we share that fear with the animals at our core even though we have learned to cover it up through clever stratagems. The sense of ease in Sengcan's poem represents the soothing of this fundamental fear.

It may be that in order to effectively translate the sentiments of the poem into our own lives we need to take a much closer look at just how fragmented our lives have become. Only then the task of repairing our fragmentation can perhaps begin anew. In our own particular ways we all wish to be at ease and we all wish to be protected. How we create a mindset and a way of being that offers the sense of ease and protection in a very complex world is indeed our challenge. The challenge is huge, and to try to gloss over it or marginalize it through simplistic slogans would be a disservice to our own intelligence and harmful to our well-being. The pithy sayings in *Trust in Mind* may

look like slogans but each one is a profound pointer to the working of human
mind. The intention of this commentary is to explore those hidden layers.

I have tried to walk a very fine line in this commentary. I have not privi-
leged either the ancestor-lineage-historical Zen or the "feel-good" inter-
pretation of popular Zen in America. My hope is that in this commentary the
classical teachings of the Buddha provide a new context to the Chan
approach to liberation, and create a somewhat different reading of Chan for
our own time and place, one that I hope transcends any narrow ideology.
The issue is liberation through practice, not the privileging of one view-
point over the other. The challenge in writing about Chan and Buddhist
teachings is the care that needs to be taken in transporting a "zendo under-
standing" (that is, insights gained in intensive meditation training through
talks by teachers as well as one's own going deep within) to a "library under-
standing" (the premise that linguistic modalities of knowing will yield lib-
erative insights). My hope is that this commentary will inspire readers to
move from a library understanding to a zendo understanding. For truly,
without some training in how our own mind works through formal medi-
tation retreats, all our understanding about Chan and the sentiments of *Trust
in Mind* are likely to remain at the level of mere coffeehouse discussion.

A word of caution, I believe, is in order in reading an ancient text from a
different culture. It is not uncommon for those getting introduced to Zen
to worry that through Zen practice they might somehow become zombies
or robots. The premises of the Chan approach to life, especially as high-
lighted in *Xinxinming*, are indeed much at odds with the Western idea of
what it means to be a fully integrated human being, but they do not seek to
reverse the millennia of biological evolution made in the development of
the neocortex in the modern human brain. If anything, they point out that
there is a civilizational responsibility for building upon these gains by giv-
ing up the imperatives of aggression and violence that have been a marked
feature for nearly all of recorded human history. The destruction of human
life through war and genocide in the twentieth century alone is enough to
make a sane person question whether we have "evolved" as much as we like
to claim. *Trust in Mind* asks us to match our conduct with that claim.

In the best sense of the term, Chan and Buddhist teachings offer an alter-
nate worldview. To enter fully into this, or any other, alternative worldview
requires a willingness to examine our own existing worldview and in all hon-
esty assess whether it contributes to a sense of being at ease in the world.

More and more, in a technological society, human beings are trained to be interchangeable parts of a giant machine called "the economic system." To enter into the world of Chan is to recover our humanity that has been lost in our designation as an interchangeable part in the machine. The ultimate issue is not Chan itself but the death of all that is human when individuals become nothing more than a cog in the wheel. We need some models, some inspirations to recover our humanity. In the contemporary West, especially in America, the mindset is to try to change the world according to our personal agenda, our own idea of how it should be. The Buddhist model is to try to change ourselves in ways that are optimally beneficial and nonharming to us and to others. This in no way means becoming callous or ignorant but involves a larger civilizational perspective that any genuine change must involve real human beings and their personal sense of ease or dis-ease in the world. The political, the social, and the religious must be in the service of this sense of ease, rather than function as coercive ideologies.

My sense of Sengcan's poem is that it is one of those rare texts that speak to each individual in each generation in a very personal way. It invites each person to offer his or her own commentary on the poem based on personal life experience. And I hope that this present book will provoke the reader into doing just that, and therein will lie the poem's greatest value. What has been said of Zhuangzi remains equally true of Sengcan and his poem:

> Like all immortals, Chuang wrote for his contemporaries and not with one eye on the future. But he is as modern as tomorrow. Every reading rewards us in some fashion, re-reading deepens understanding, and reflection enlarges our consciousness. Like a fine art, or the Tao itself, this classic can never be mastered, only participated in.... We whose inheritance stems from Euclidian concepts and Greek ideas are always challenged by the paradoxes that lie in wait for us in Chinese concepts. We usually translate *wu wei* as no-mind or mindlessness. But this is a state that only results after having "minded" greatly, of having labored to reach a point.... This inaction results from the proper use of action.

Many of us are caught up in ideas similar to Chuang's because the pressures that weigh upon us are similar, and we too face difficult moral choices. We are accordion-pleated by the timelessness of time until we stand side by side with Zhuangzi. Then we can be grateful that occasionally, even out of periods of disorder and chaos, a great work can not only emerge—it can endure.[7]

This book is structured so that the chapter "The Dharma of Trust in Mind" provides a historical and doctrinal background of Indian Buddhism embedded in the poem; the chapter "The Tao of Trust in Mind" provides the Taoist background of the poem, and the chapter "The Chan of Trust in Mind" provides, likewise, the Chan background. Together, these three chapters provide the reader with a full historical and doctrinal context of the poem. I happen to believe that no other Zen text delivers the semiotics of Buddho-Taoism in its formative stage in quite the same way as does *Xinxinming*. Hence its continued appreciation in our own time and place.

The second part of the book is a personal exploration of each line of the poem, which could also be read as a stand-alone commentary.

A Note on the Translation

There are many translations of Sengcan's poem. I have used the translation by Richard B. Clarke in the main commentary because of its accessibility and expressiveness. The other translations are by Sheng-yen ("Trust in Mind" in *The Poetry of Enlightenment*); R. H. Blyth ("The Hsinhsinming" in *Zen and Zen Classics*, vol. 1); D. T. Suzuki ("Inscribed on the Believing Mind" in *Essays in Zen Buddhism*); Arthur Waley ("On Trust in the Heart" in *Buddhist Texts Through the Ages*); Lu Kuan Yu ("Have Faith in Your Mind" in *Practical Buddhism*); Stanley Lombardo ("Trusting in Mind" in *Primary Point* magazine); and a recent translation by Philip Dunn and Peter Jourdan ("A Song of Enlightenment" in *The Book of Nothing*). The Lombardo translation is a poetic and concise translation; Lu Kuan Yu's translation is highly idiosyncratic and has a different feeling-tone from other translations; the Dunn and Jourdan translation is quite free-form and highly poetic. In one of the translations of the poem, by the Zen Buddhist Order of Hsu Yun, the word Great Way in the first line has been replaced by Buddha Mind. In doing so, this translation replaces the Taoist flavor of Sengcan's original with a more explicit Buddhist religiosity. I have included this translation here as well, in the appendix, to provide a contrast. The Clarke translation appears at the beginning of chapter 1. I have also created an appendix where other translations have been put alongside the Clarke translation to show the reader the wide range of interpretations in which these words from the Chinese have been understood in the last few generations.

In the main commentary, where necessary I have mentioned other translations that might perhaps speak to the line in question with greater clarity or emphasis. The Chinese language leaves itself open to many different translative endeavors in European languages; my attempt here is to provide as much clarity as possible while working with this medieval Chinese text.

Sheng-yen also has a commentary on the poem, published as *Trust in Mind: A Guide to Chan Practice*. As the author himself notes,

> Since the talks [on which the volume is based] were given within the context of intensive meditation practice, I did not adopt a scholarly point of view or analytical approach. It is not a formal commentary on the text; rather, I use the poem as a taking-off point to inspire the practitioner and deal with certain issues that arise during the course of practice.[8]

Dennis Genpo Merzel, a contemporary American Zen teacher, has offered a similar commentary based on his retreat talks (in *The Eye Never Sleeps*). He has also used the Clarke translation, and his commentary is restricted by its need to function as exhortation to practitioners within a Zen retreat. The preface to his book has a useful referencing by Hakuyu Taizan Maezumi to various commentaries on the text in medieval China and Japan.

R. H. Blyth, the least-acknowledged guiding spirit of Western understanding of Zen, has a most unusual and eccentric commentary (which perfectly captures Blyth's persona of a "Zen fool") in the first volume of *Zen and Zen Classics*. He brings in Shakespeare and Marcus Aurelius and Thoreau in delightful and seamless ways. His is the spirit of the poet, the scholar, and Zen eccentric, all combined in one extraordinary package.

Dusan Pajin of Belgrade University, Yugoslavia, has a textual analysis of Chinese characters used in the poem that appears as "On Faith in Mind" in *Journal of Oriental Studies*, vol. XXVI, no. 2.

My own attempt has been to provide a thorough historical and doctrinal context to the poem as well as practice perspectives for a well-informed Chan/Zen practitioner who has some interest in the issues of delusion and liberation as they have been explored in that tradition. In doing so, this commentary departs significantly from the commentaries of Sheng-yen, Merzel, Blyth, and Pajin. I hope the theses of this book are acceptable to the scholar just as the perspectives here are helpful to the practitioners.

≪ Trust in Mind: The Poem ≫

⬥ Xinxinming ⬥

TRANSLATED BY RICHARD B. CLARKE

The Great Way is not difficult
for those who have no preferences.
When love and hate are both absent
everything becomes clear and undisguised.
Make the smallest distinction, however,
and heaven and earth are set infinitely apart.
If you wish to see the truth,
then hold no opinions for or against anything.
To set up what you like against what you dislike
is the disease of the mind.
When the deep meaning of things is not understood,
the mind's essential peace is disturbed to no avail.
The Way is perfect like vast space
where nothing is lacking and nothing is in excess.
Indeed, it is due to our choosing to accept or reject
that we do not see the true nature of things.
Live neither in the entanglements of outer things,
nor in inner feelings of emptiness.
Be serene in the oneness of things
and such erroneous views will disappear by themselves.
When you try to stop activity to achieve passivity,
your very effort fills you with activity.
As long as you remain in one extreme or the other,
you will never know Oneness.
Those who do not live in the single Way
fail in both activity and passivity,
assertion and denial.

To deny the reality of things
is to miss their reality;
to assert the emptiness of things is to miss their reality.
The more you talk and think about it,
the further astray you wander from the truth.
Stop talking and thinking,
and there is nothing you will not be able to know.
To return to the root is to find the meaning,
but to pursue appearances is to miss the source.
At the moment of inner enlightenment,
there is a going beyond appearance and emptiness.
The changes that appear to occur in the empty world
we call real only because of our ignorance.
Do not search for the truth;
only cease to cherish opinions.
Do not remain in the dualistic state;
avoid such pursuits carefully.
If there is even a trace of this and that, of right
     and wrong,
the Mind-essence will be lost in confusion.
Although all dualities come from the One,
do not be attached even to this One.
When the mind exists undisturbed in the Way,
nothing in the world can offend,
and when a thing can no longer offend, it ceases to exist
     in the old way.
When no discriminating thoughts arise, the old mind
     ceases to exist.
When thought objects vanish, the thinking subject
     vanishes,
as when the mind vanishes, objects vanish.
Things are objects because of the subject (mind);
the mind (subject) is such because of things (objects).
Understand the relativity of these two
and the basic reality: the unity of emptiness.
In this Emptiness the two are indistinguishable,
and each contains in itself the whole world.

If you do not discriminate between coarse and fine,
you will not be tempted to prejudice and opinion.
To live in the Great Way is neither easy nor difficult,
but those with limited views are fearful and irresolute:
    the faster they hurry, the slower they go,
and clinging cannot be limited; and
even to be attached to the idea of enlightenment
    is to go astray.
Just let things be in their own way,
and there will be neither coming nor going.
Obey the nature of things (your own nature),
and you will walk freely and undisturbed.
When thought is in bondage the truth is hidden,
for everything is murky and unclear,
and the burdensome practice of judging brings
    annoyance and weariness.
What benefit can be derived from distinctions and
    separations?
If you wish to move in the One Way
do not dislike even the world of senses and ideas.
Indeed, to accept them fully
is identical with true Enlightenment.
The wise person strives to no goals
but the foolish person fetters himself.
This is one Dharma, not many; distinctions arise
from the clinging needs of the ignorant.
To seek Mind with the (discriminating) mind
is the greatest of all mistakes.
Rest and unrest derive from illusion;
with enlightenment there is no liking or disliking.
All dualities come from
ignorant inference; they are like dreams of
    flowers in the air:
foolish to try to grasp them.
Gain and loss, right and wrong:
such thoughts must finally be abolished at once.
If the eye never sleeps,

all dreams will naturally cease.
If the mind makes no discriminations,
the ten thousand things are as they are, of single essence.
To understand the mystery of this One-essence
is to be released from all entanglements.
When all things are seen equally
the timeless Self-essence is reached.
No comparisons or analogies are possible
in this causeless, relationless state.
Consider movement stationary and the stationary
    in motion,
both movement and rest disappear.
When such dualities cease to exist
Oneness itself cannot exist.
To this ultimate finality
no law or description applies.
For the unified mind in accord with the Way
all self-centered straining ceases.
Doubts and irresolutions vanish
and life in true faith is possible.
With a single stroke we are freed from bondage;
nothing clings to us and we hold to nothing.
All is empty, clear, self-illuminating,
with no exertion of the mind's power.
Here thought, feeling, knowledge, and imagination
are of no value.
In this world of suchness
there is neither self nor other-than-self.
To come directly into harmony with this reality,
just simply say when doubt arises, "Not two."
In this "not two" nothing is separate,
nothing excluded.
No matter when or where,
enlightenment means entering this truth.
And this truth is beyond extension or diminution in time
    or space;
in it a single thought is ten thousand years.

Emptiness here, emptiness there,
but the infinite universe stands always before your eyes.
Infinitely large and infinitely small;
no difference, for definitions have vanished
and no boundaries are seen.
So too with Being and non-Being.
Don't waste time in doubts and arguments
that have nothing to do with this.
One thing, all things:
move among and intermingle, without distinction.
To live in this realization
is to be without anxiety about non-perfection.
To live in this faith is the road to nonduality,
because the nondual is one with the trusting mind.
Words! The Way is beyond language,
for in it there is no yesterday, no tomorrow, no today.

PART ONE

1. The Dharma of Trust in Mind

THE CENTRAL CONCERN in Buddha's teachings is liberation from the confusion and craving that generate stress, dis-ease, and anguish. The first noble truth speaks of this anguish as the observation that the human condition is characterized by "dukkha." *Dukkha* is one of those key terms whose misunderstanding leads to a skewed understanding of the entire tradition. When the first noble truth is translated as "life is suffering," as many commentators have done, it comes across as an ideological statement to be posted against other ideological statements. Partisan ideologues have jumped on this mistranslation and accused Buddhist teachings of being pessimistic, or even nihilistic. But *dukkha* is more properly translated as a sense of unsatisfactoriness, unease, stress, alienation, anguish, all of which indicate the concrete experience of quantifiable psychological or physiological stresses. The Pali texts record the Buddha as saying, *"sabbe sankhara dukkha,"* literally meaning, "all formations have the characteristics of dukkha." However we translate the term *dukkha,* nowhere in Buddhist canon do we find the broad declaration that "life is suffering." If we can tear ourselves away from the non-issues generated by the mistranslation of "life is suffering," we find that Buddha's teachings, at their core, are addressed to *sankharas*—mental formations or constructions. As such, the teachings are psychological and existential guides, rather than a broad metaphysical declaration about "life" being one way or another.

The associated teachings of *sabbe sankhara anicca / sabbe dhamma anatta* ("all constructions have the nature of impermanence / all phenomena have the nature of nonself") complete a core tripartite template unique to the Buddha. What this template makes clear is that while the attributes of impermanence and nonself may be a feature of all constructions, dukkha is very much a psychological feature resulting from our relationship to those

constructions. A misperception of constructions having qualities of perma-
nence and an abiding substance would inevitably result in a skewed rela-
tionship with them. It is not too much of a doctrinal jump to claim that the
Buddha's main enterprise was to speak to these skewed relationships rather
than to constructions themselves. The sense of dukkha, of unsatisfactori-
ness, is obtained in the skewed relationships rather than in constructions
themselves, which is to say that things of the world are not in and of them-
selves good or bad.

It is important to note here that given the patterns of Indian philosophy,
there is a sense that samsara, the world of constructions, is undesirable and is
not something to be chased after. When the mindset becomes rigidly religious,
as it often does in Brahmanical Hinduism, the assumption still is that samsara
and its components are in and of themselves somehow flawed. The danger in
religious rigidity is that it can lead to a metaphysical position or an ideologi-
cal rejection of samsara rather than a sober reflection on one's own skewed
relationship to samsara and on the anguish that comes out of that relationship.

When the poem *Trust in Mind* mentions "dualities," it is precisely address-
ing the skewed relationships to which the Buddha's first noble truth is point-
ing, thus making *dukkha* a relational quality rather than a metaphysical
equation against which other metaphysical equations may or must be pitted.
The first noble truth is an invitation to explore our own personal, human
experience and see that we have constructed our own world of experience
and that we have constructed relationships with that world, and further-
more that both these constructions lead to dukkha.

Thus has Buddha diagnosed the ailing human condition. He then offers a
cure for that ailment, a Way or Path in which the sense of anguish is replaced
by one of being at ease, of making peace with ourselves and the world. This
is done not by trying to change the world according to our own neuroses or
small-minded needs but repairing or reestablishing a different kind of rela-
tionship with it.

Problems arise when Buddhist teachings are seen through a lens that pre-
sumes there must be a "search" for happiness. A fuller discussion of happi-
ness, at least as understood in the Western philosophical tradition is beyond
the scope of this chapter, but suffice it to say that in the West, "happiness"
is a positive condition with identifiable cultural components. The classical
Buddhist tradition (by which I mean the Indian Pali and Sanskrit traditions)
does not talk about happiness in direct, positivistic ways but rather implies

that happiness is the *absence* of *dukkha*, a "natural" state free from alienation, stress, unsatisfactoriness, and anguish.

This understanding of "happiness" is perhaps best described with a metaphor. Imagine clenching your fist very tightly for a very long time. Though you may not experience pain at first, it will gradually become more and more uncomfortable as the muscles tense and cramp. But when you simply open your hand, releasing the muscles and the tension, the constrictive pain and discomfort is gone.

In our daily experience we clench our fist around our ideas of self and the world, and in due course our experience becomes unbearably painful. Our behavior reflects our attempt to get out of that pain but by that time we have forgotten to open up the fist.

The sense of ease in the *Xinxinmng* finds its pedigree in what I would provisionally call the "optimal life" alluded to by the Buddha. For people who have not yet had an awakening or enlightenment experience, and for those (such as the Buddha) who have, the question still remains: How should one live one's life? The Buddha's eightfold path is the roadmap to both the pre-awakening and post-awakening modes of living. Although not directly mentioned as part of the eightfold path, the four qualities of heart and mind called the *brahma viharas* (translated as "divine abodes" or "sublime states of mind") have always been crucial. These four sublime states are: loving-kindness *(metta)*, the practice of which counteracts anger and ill-will, and wishes for others to be happy; compassion *(karuna)*, which provides the remedy for cruelty and wishes for others to be free from suffering; appreciative or sympathetic joy *(mudita)*, curative for jealousy and envy; and equanimity *(upekkha)*, which dissolves clinging and attachment, as well as extremes of reaction. While the first three qualities are proactive contemplative practices, equanimity is the condition that becomes the underlying structural grid, so to speak, of the optimal life. There is an intimate and organic link between Sengcan's sentiments in *Trust in Mind* and the way in which equanimity is understood in the classical tradition.

The Theravadan monk Bhikkhu Bodhi, one of the leading modern scholars and translators of Pali texts, argues that after six years of extreme ascetic practices, Buddha's search took an altogether new turn:

> He went back to the contemplations [practices that sought to transcend all sensory experience] but made a radical change in the

technique. Instead of looking for an ultimate truth, he focused on rendering the contemplative process more morally oriented. He therefore decided that the initial state of contemplation is one in which a person has to refrain from pleasures of sense and unwholesome tendencies. This enabled him to enjoy a state of joy and happiness qualitatively different from those associated with pleasures of sense. This sharpened his reflective *(vitakka)* and investigative *(vicara)* capacities. If the last two were to be pursued without limitations, he would have struggled to unravel the origin of the universe through reflection and to search for an ultimate reality through investigation. Realizing the danger, he temporarily suspended reflection and investigation. This left him with a serene feeling of joy and happiness. However, such joy and happiness could lead to obsessions that becloud one's perception. Hence his decision to suspend joy and happiness. The resulting state was one of the clear, unprejudiced perception.

The Buddha used a term of rare occurrence in the pre-Buddhist languages in India, namely, *upekkha* (Sk. *upeksha*, a word formed out of *upa+iks*, meaning "taking a close look"). It is generally rendered into English as "equanimity," a term of more ethical import, but which highlights the epistemological stance, hence better translated as "consideration." This is because a prejudiced mind, a mind that has already been made up, cannot consider anything that is contrary to its accepted views. Hence, a "considering mind" beautifully defined as one which has become pliable *(kammaniya)*, become stable *(thita)*, become flexible *(mudubhuta)* and reached a state of not fluttering *(anenjapatta)*. This is a concentrated mind *(samahita)*, without blemish *(anagana)*, purified *(parisuddha)* and cleansed *(pariyodata)* with all defiling tendencies gone *(vigatupakkilesa)*. It is almost difficult to think of the salutary effects of adopting such a perspective in the investigative processes relating to science, technology, medicine, economics, political science and sociology to mention a few. This is especially so in the context of the modern world where all such disciplines are based upon the inflexible and rigid dichotomies such as the true and false, the existent and the non-existent. Absolutism of some sort is the inevitable result.

The good and the peaceful that he attained under the Bodhi tree permeated all his teachings, whether they pertain to explanations of the physical or objective world, the human personality, social, political and moral life as well as the use of the most important method of communication, namely, language.[9]

This explanation by Bhikkhu Bodhi becomes, in turn, a guiding tool for us in any consideration of what Sengcan might mean by the nondual or One Mind. Neither the Buddha nor Sengcan seem interested in establishing an ontology leading to an affirmation or absolutism of one kind or another. What they seem interested in is pointing to an equanimous mind which is a quality of being in the world in which the mind has become pliable, stable, flexible, not fluttering, concentrated, without blemish, purified, cleansed, and free of all defiling tendencies. This is the awakened mind and the resulting functioning state of such a mind is one of clear, unprejudiced perception. This is the "good and the peaceful" attained by the Buddha under the Bodhi tree.

Upekkha is also translated as equipoise, a state of balance that is both stable and flexible. *Visuddhimagga*, the classical compendium of Theravada teachings, defines *upekkha* in this way:

Equanimity is characterized as promoting the aspect of neutrality towards beings. Its function is to see equality in beings. It is manifested as the quieting of resentment and approval. Its proximate cause is seeing ownership of deeds *(kamma)* thus: "Beings are owners of their deeds. Whose [if not theirs] is the choice by which they will become happy, or will get free from suffering ..." It succeeds when it makes resentment and approval subside.[10]

And this is what Sengcan's poem is asking us to cultivate: to not live our life through resentment or approval, or other kinds of dualities. Equanimity is a state of mind in which both concentration and mindfulness are present to the highest degree; the presence of these two qualities is the foundation for

...developing insight—tuning in to the busy highways of the body and mind, the arising and passing away of sense stimuli through the six senses. When we don't have that equanimity, the mind is easily disturbed and distracted by pleasant and painful impingements, perceptions, and thoughts, all of which slow down and impede the progress of insight.[11]

So, true happiness in the Buddhist sense is neither esoteric nor based on any outside source; it is entirely the result of self-cultivation. Both Taoist and Chan traditions warn that this self-cultivation must be self-inspiring and coming from a place of self-knowing rather than something obsessional. If one contextualizes one's self-cultivation through a deep immersion in the teachings of *dukkha, anitya, and anatman,* self-cultivation becomes an open-ended process rather than a goal that one pursues as an agenda.

Sengcan's poem conveys a mood of equanimity without the jargon of religious terms—but the absence of such terms in no way diminishes the illuminative nature of that mood which is itself synonymous with liberation or enlightenment.

The first noble truth is a recognition that dukkha or the sense of incompleteness is a result of our obsession with trying to "fix" the world around us according to our preferences. Over time, this creates a highly constricted feedback loop in which self-referentiality feeds upon another layer of self-referentiality. If, for example, the first layer of reality-construction "I am X" is followed immediately by the second and third layers of "*I* am Y" and "I am not Z," we soon enter into a multiplicity of identities determined by the nature of X, Y, and Z without ever clarifying the nature of "I" itself. In these proliferations, the "I" is always confused about its own identity and its relationship to X, Y, and Z at various levels of alienation. In a highly technologized society such as ours, for instance, in a race to live longer and healthier we are at the same time losing track of the question of why we are trying to live longer. Forgetfulness becomes a fuel for consumerism, and consumerism becomes a breeding ground for forgetfulness. Consuming without knowing why—or even what—we are consuming becomes a recipe for alienation from our deepest source of well-being.

The issue in the Buddha's teachings is not how long one lives (according to legend, Ananda, the Buddha's sole companion in his last moments, urged him to live much longer beyond his earthbound eighty years), but how one meets the challenges of living, aging, becoming sick, and dying. We are encouraged to face these four inevitabilities without vexations, and perhaps even be motivated by them to strive for liberation. Even allowing for the hypothetical situation that some rare yogic master sequestered in a high Himalayan cave is able to live, say, for a thousand years—such an endeavor and lifestyle is a result of extremely hard work that the average person is neither willing nor able to do. And so, the hypothetical hermit-yogi notwithstanding, the rest of us still have to age, become sick, and die. This is the ultimate challenge of human existence, and this is the challenge that the Buddha sought to address. Yet in even this ordinary human life we do have options: we can live with a hankering for life as an endless carnival, or we can with full awareness let go of all clinging. It is this latter choice that the poem *Trust in Mind* suggests.

It is a commonplace understanding in the Buddhist, and the larger Indian philosophical tradition, that any time we state things positively we are making an ideological statement, and thereby assume the burden of proof. Human nature, being what it is, we are conditioned to identify with this or that and because of this need for identification, we have the associated need of further defining, at a secondary but unconscious level according to our emotional and psychological needs. Psychologists call it projection. We live most of our lives under the assumption that our projections are really "real" rather than mental constructions we ourselves have created. In our daily language, for example, we use the word *God* a lot and assume that in our conversations with other people there is a common agreement as to what this word means. But each person's understanding of God is probably slightly or even massively different and, when pressed, we discover, that we are projecting a lot of our own unexamined and positivistic assumptions onto this linguistic term. By contrast, in the Madhyamika tradition of Indian Mahayana as well as in Chan, when things are stated negatively, it is a call for (a) looking at our own personal experience; and (b) being aware of how language shapes our understanding of experience. When the Heart Sutra, for example, declares, "There is no attainment, with nothing to attain," it challenges some very fundamental assumptions we have about ourselves and our "spiritual" practice because we want to be able to show *something* for our *effort*. Any idea of attainment or effort becomes a palliative for self-referentiality. A categorical assertion such as "attainment" implies that there are identifiable components that can be the subject of explication and agreement. But whatever agreements we can reach, these are social agreements rather than revealing the true nature of the assertion itself.

In our pure, pre-linguistic experience we don't experience the language-based categories of "suffering" or "happiness." We experience stresses and tensions; we experience a sense of wellness or relaxation. These are experienced as sensations in the body and mind rather than categories of ontology; "body" and mind" are experienced as constricted or easeful spaces. The fallacy of using language to describe human experience in broad general categories like "suffering" or "happiness" is likely to turn them into metaphysical or ideological statements that many traditions take for granted. A worldview based on these linguistic categories becomes a roadblock to exploring what's happening in the mind-body system at any given time. When we explore this in a disciplined manner, say, in a meditation retreat, all our worldviews become porous and ultimately unsustainable in the face of pre-linguistic experiencing of mind and body. Life itself is seen as relational in the sense of a causal network, and deeply interwoven into the fabric of everything that lives and breathes, rather than an abstract philosophical proposition.

The Buddha's diagnosis of the causes of dukkha as a relational quality in our lives is *avijja* (delusion, confusion, misperception); delusion or confusion as to the nature of the world which is both *anitya* (impermanent) and *anatman* (insubstantial). The existentially painful human condition, in the Buddha's observation, is a case of misperception on the part of the perceiver, and leads to clinging to things that basically have the nature of impermanence and insubstantiality. The cure then is to find the corrective lens through which to perceive the world without distortion. This corrective lens has less to do with establishing qualifications or components in objects of perceptions than with the relational quality one establishes with things that are impermanent and insubstantial. We make emotional and psychological investments in things based on a misguided notion that things are somehow stable and will abide unchanged in time and space. When we find out that our investment is not working according to our calculations, we are overtaken by grief and lament.

The Buddha's second noble truth, and the twelve links of dependent arising outlined therein, speaks eloquently of how we put into place a system of making psychological and emotional investment in things of the world. This dependent arising (Pali: *paticcasamuppada*) has been commented upon in depth by a number of contemporary writers. Here I only want to point out the twelve links of dependent-arising to those readers who may not be familiar with them rather than undertake a detailed or systematic study of this core teaching (Pali terms appear below in parentheses):

1. delusion/confusion *(avijja)* is a precondition for
2. mental formations/constructions *(sankhara)*, which is a precondition for
3. consciousness *(vinnana)*, which is a precondition for
4. name and form *(nama-rupa)*, which is a precondition for
5. the six senses including mind *(salayatana)*, which are a precondition for
6. contact *(phassa)*, which is a precondition for
7. feeling *(vedana)*, which is a precondition for
8. longing *(tanha)*, which is a precondition for
9. clinging *(upadana)*, which is a precondition for
10. becoming *(bhava)*, which is a precondition for
11. rebirthing *(jati)*, which is a precondition for
12. aging and dying *(jara-marana)*

Of these, the links of longing, clinging, and becoming (8, 9, 10) form a subset that speaks eloquently to the human existential and psychological condition. The Buddha was the first religious thinker to speak of the causal links of dependent arising of suffering within the human mind and it sets him apart as a humanist thinker, first and foremost. In my own reading, all Buddhist teachings, at their core, speak of this longing-clinging-becoming and its causes and cure. The entirety of the rest of all the Buddhist traditions can be viewed as a footnote to the causes and cure of longing-clinging-becoming. To paraphrase numerous Zen masters: Once you get it—and it's not all that complicated—the only thing left to do is to be in the world in such a way that the workings of longing-clinging-becoming do not continue to operate in your psyche in the same way. This is the model of the *arahant*, the liberated being, in Pali tradition. This is also the basic model that the bodhisattva of the Mahayana tradition builds upon. (Contrary to common understanding, the bodhisattva model never rejected the arahant model but simply expanded it.)

Trust in Mind speaks to this making-of-the-liberated-being in a slightly different language, and slightly different doctrinal context than Indian Mahayana Buddhism. By conflating the Taoist idea of a sage (which will be elaborated upon in the next chapter) it creates a new model of the Buddhist sage than the one that appears in Indian Buddhist literature. The specifically Chan configuration of the sage, drawing upon both the Indian Buddhist and the Chinese Taoist models, is that s/he is always in the service of a liberation in the world, here and now. If all of *dukkha* comes from unexamined or mis-construed longings and sets into motion a chain of unexamined clinging and equally unexamined becoming, the task then is to correct what has been misconstrued, and live in a way in which we are constantly aware of the neg-ative impact of these misconstrued longings-clingings-becomings.

A proper understanding of the term *bhava* (the tenth link in the chain of dependent arising) then becomes critical to the subset we are talking about. *Bhava*, in Pali and Sanskrit, can be translated as both "being" and "becom-ing," depending on the context. In the Western philosophical tradition, these may be two separate categories, and may involve two different methodologies of understanding, but that distinction is not present in Buddhist languages. In the West, all speculations about the nature of "Being" (often capitalized!) have given rise to numerous unresolved meta-physical debates. By contrast, in Buddhist teachings an act of being is an act of becoming; Being itself is becoming, and becoming itself is being.

If the entire construct (whether psychological or phenomenological) is impermanent, it would follow that it is not a fruitful exercise to posit a "Being" in the construct because "Being" implies a sense of continuity out-side of time and space in an unchanged fashion. But if the construct is under-going constant change and revision, it would also follow that this construct is not the same as it was in the previous moment, nor will it be the same in the next moment. Thus, definitionally, the construct is a "becoming" and is always in the process of becoming. At the same time, for a brief moment when the construct is the object of perception, we may assign to it a provi-sional quality of "being" (not "Being"!) if only as a frame of reference for what has been and what will be. If we understand correctly that the being of each moment (which is always the present moment) is also its becoming, we also understand the becoming of that provisional being in the past and future moments.

A proper understanding of *bhava* therefore is "being-in-becoming." (In each moment of human experience there is a subject (being) impacted upon by the sensory input from the environment and being changed by it (becom-ing) and thus in each moment there is always a subject in the process of being reconfigured, however slightly or subtly. A thought, for example, is not a simple event happening statically to a thinker. It is changing the thinker by its impact and since the thinker has thought the thought in the first place, the thinker (being) *is* the thought (becoming) itself, and thought itself is the thinker. The two are an inseparable process rather than two distinct entities. A proper designation perhaps is "thinker-in-thoughting.) This understanding of "being-in-becoming" takes us away from the misperception that there is a "Being" who experiences "becoming." While the Buddha refused to take a metaphysical position on whether or not there was a "Being" outside the process of becoming, the sense of the teaching of *anatman*, or nonself, is really a lack of a Being outside the present moment of being-in-becoming. Being-in-becoming becomes an entirely experiential, self-contained posture that does not need any metaphysical speculation for its manifestation. When Being-in-becoming operates through longing and clinging, it gives rise to confusion and unsatisfactoriness; when it operates through conscious release of clinging, it give rise to a sense of ease in the world of becoming without requiring a notion of a Being.

The cessation of clinging is one of the central themes of Buddha's teachings. An alternative metaphor to the unclasping of the fist is the image of pulling your hand out of the fire—obviously this is a less painful experience than keeping your hand in the fire. Again and again, the Buddha addressed himself to the issue of nonclinging, of letting go. His teaching was addressed to the ascetics who had already left home, and had some taste of the pain that comes from entanglements of the world. It is within the context of this taste of pain issuing out of entanglements that the Buddha's teachings of nonclinging were most effective.

The dialectic of Middle Way was first used by Nagarjuna, the founder of the Madhyamika school of Indian Mahayana in the second century, to further expand the argument for nonclinging. The centerpiece of Nagarjuna's dialectic is *shunyata* or "emptiness." When Sengcan uses the term *emptiness* repeatedly in *Trust in Mind*, it is functionally a reworking of Nagarjuna's dialectic of shunyata in a Buddho-Taoist framework. Nagarjuna points out that because things arise in dependence on other things (this is the truth of dependent-arising) they have no own-being *(svabhava)* of their own; things are empty of own-being. Though it is present in early Pali texts in an embryonic form, Nagarjuna's dialectic defined shunyata as the core wisdom teaching of the Buddha, and brought about a philosophical revolution in Buddhist tradition.

In order for his dialectic to work as a tool for nonclinging, Nagarjuna elaborated upon the "theory of two truths" that was already present in some embryonic form in the early tradition: the absolute (Pali: *paramatthasacca*; Sanskrit: *paramartha-satya*) and the provisional (Pali: *sammutisacca*; Sanskrit: *samvriti-satya*). The absolute truth of things is that they are empty of own-being; their provisional truth is that they exist, even though this existence is momentary and fleeting. The absolute is not the denial of the existence of things; the provisional is not an affirmation of any inherent substance or own-being. The purpose of meditation practice or investigative insight is to perceive the absolute nature of things while immersed in countless encounters with their provisional appearances. It is only through this lens of perception that nonclinging works as a tool for liberation.

The challenge in reading Nagarjuna and Madhyamika dialectic is to not absolutize the truth that they speak of. The "truth" being offered for consideration is merely a skillful methodology for nonclinging, rather than putting into place any metaphysical ideology. The Buddhist thinkers of early medieval India, roughly the period of the third to the eighth centuries were keenly aware of this danger and worked assiduously to avoid it; they spoke of the "emptiness of emptiness" and seem to have implied emptiness of emptiness of emptiness *ad nauseum*. Tsongkhapa (1357–1419), the founder of the Gelug school of Tibetan Buddhism and one of the greatest thinkers in Buddhist history, wrote his masterpiece, *The Essence of Eloquent Speech*, equating dependent-arising with emptiness. Like every major Mahayana thinker, he builds upon the arguments first proposed by Nagarjuna in his Madhyamika approach. A commentary on Tsongkhapa's work by Lobsang Gyatso *(The Harmony of Emptiness and Dependent-Arising)* offers carefully constructed arguments on this conflation.

What becomes important is to keep in mind that when the "absolute" of shunyata is talked about, it is a heuristic device for investigative purposes rather than a metaphysical proposition. Thorough intellectual investigation allows one to infer the absolute truth of shunyata (the ultimate nature of things) through the dialectic of Nagarjuna, Tsongkhapa, and other Buddhist philosophers. (A sustained meditative inquiry can yield the same result in a more direct way).

The core issue, then, is the ultimate nature of things: appearance versus reality; contingent versus the absolute. Sengcan comes back to this issue again and again in his poem. For the Buddha nonclinging was not a mere philosophical issue; for him nonclinging naturally arises when the ultimate nature of things is clearly understood and life is lived out of that understanding.

We may wonder how forms sustain themselves within the world of form. For the Buddhist thinkers the issue is not the "substance" of things but their fleeting temporal and spatial functioning; forms arise dependently upon numerous causes and conditions, and function only so long as the underlying structure of causes and conditions remains in place. In and of themselves, forms have no own-being *(svabhava)*. Because the underlying causes and conditions are themselves in a process of continuous change, the "existence" of appearances/forms is changing accordingly, leading to the insight that "existence" is not a stable phenomenon in time or space. Hence "existence," while provisionally functional, has no own-being and should be recognized as such.

The issues of appearance versus reality, conventional versus absolute truth, are captured marvelously and familiarly in the Heart Sutra (the *Prajnaparamita Hridaya Sutra*), a core text of the Mahayana tradition. It celebrates the teaching of shunyata, and in my own commentaries on the Heart Sutra and Diamond Sutra, I have tried to present to the contemporary reader a framework for a comprehensive understanding of this vivid teaching. Rather than repeat those arguments here, I have put them as an appendix in the back of this book for those who wish to peruse them. Here I want to focus primarily on two contemporary Buddhist thinkers who have spoken eloquently on shunyata and whose writings allow us to enter the world of Sengcan's *Trust in Mind* with ease.

Nagarjuna's dialectic has recently been re-rendered poetically by Stephen Batchelor in his *Verses from the Center: A Buddhist Vision of the Sublime*. He writes,

Recognizing mental and physical processes as "empty" of self was, for the Buddha, the way to dispel the confusion that lies at the origin of anguish, for such confusion configures a sense of self as a fixed and opaque thing that feels disconnected from the dynamic, contingent and fluid processes of life. Emptiness does not deny these vital processes. It challenges the insistent fixation about self that obscures them, thus rendering life flat, frustrating and repetitive. Emptiness is a cipher of freedom... Rather than something to understand, emptiness is a condition in which one aspires to

live... Living in emptiness is equivalent to following the path to
awakening itself... Emptiness is a metaphor for authenticity... To
dwell in emptiness means living with the ambiguous and nondu-
alistic nature of life... While the middle way is grounded in insight
into the emptiness of self, it expands the experience of emptiness
into a sensibility that resists any attempt to pin things down to
"this" or "that."...emptiness as inseparable from the utter con-
tingency of life itself... Emptiness is not a state but a way... It is a
recovery of the freedom to configure oneself as an intentional,
unimpeded trajectory through the shifting, ambiguous sands of
life.... Emptiness is experienced as the letting go of fixed ideas
about oneself and the world...leaving nothing to hold on to.
Instead of offering the consolations of belief, he [Nagarjuna] holds
out the tantalizing possibility of freedom.[12]

Masao Abe, one of our preeminent contemporary Buddhist philosophers,
points out that shunyata is not quite the negativity the linguistic term sug-
gests: "Although the term sounds negative, it has positive religious or sote-
riological meanings."[13] Abe's position parallels the Upanishadic argument
that the methodology of *"neti, neti"* ("not this, not this") is not negative for
the sake of being negative but is in service of a truer understanding. This
truer understanding cannot be objectified or conceptualized. There is reason
to believe that the Buddha was contemporaneous with the earliest layers of
Upanishadic thought and was familiar with the negative approach. It may
even be argued that he did not see it rewarding, or intellectually compatible,
to make the jump from the negative deconstruction style of *"neti, neti"* to a
positivistic identification of the Brahman as the Universal Self, as Upan-
ishadic thinkers did. Both the Buddha and Nagarjuna seem to have been con-
tent to let the deconstruction of the *"neti, neti"* argument run to its logical
conclusion and propose that a truer understanding will emerge only when
the truth of personal experience is approached through the lens of medita-
tive inquiry (as in the case of the Buddha) or a sustained dialectic (as with
Nagarjuna). Such inquiry will reveal every experience to be impermanent
and without a substantial abiding, and when one can *trust* that insight it will
lead to a deeper place of nonverbal nonconceptualized spaciousness that is
yet a place of rest without needing any support structure. This is precisely
what Sengcan's call is in *Trust in Mind*.

The issue here is both linguistic and existential. Human experience demands a place of refuge, a place of rest, a place of ease. The response of many religious and philosophical thinkers has been to offer ever-increasingly complex categories of verbal constructs as a solace. Nonetheless human experience has consistently demonstrated that the solace of verbal constructs is insufficient to relieve suffering. *"Neti, neti"* is a deconstructive technique *par excellence* that takes us out of the trap of language, objectification, and conceptualization. But radical deconstruction by itself, undertaken as an abstract or verbal exercise, is a dead end. The Buddha used verbal constructs to speak about discernment, but also pointed out that there needs to be a corresponding *personal* experience of freedom that confirms and integrates the verbal understanding, *without depending on verbal understanding as a construct.*

What validates shunyata as a self-evident proposition is an *experiential* deconstruction of all concepts and categories, and the *existential* ease in this deconstructed space without wanting to fill it up with another construct of whatever kind. This is the core argument of *Trust in Mind*.

Martin Heidegger, one of the most influential Western philosophers of the twentieth century, has proposed creative new ways to deconstruct linguistic categories without setting up their antithetical opposites. Heidegger writes *Sein (Being)* "under erasure" as S̶e̶i̶n̶ so as to show the unobjectifiability of S̶e̶i̶n̶. Abe argues that we can also write shunyata "under erasure" i.e. sh̶u̶n̶y̶ata. This indicates that sh̶u̶n̶yata is not shunyata as we can *think* about it, but a radical deconstruction of all views that is nonetheless in service of liberation.

For Abe, there are four positive meanings of shunyata that have tremendous bearing on our understanding of the sentiments of Sengcan's *Trust in Mind*:

1. Transcending all distinctions, everything without exception is realized as it is in its suchness.

2. Shunyata is boundless openness without any center. Shunyata is free from anthropocentrism, cosmocentrism, and theocentrism. Accordingly, in shunyata there is no dominant-subordinate relationship (i.e., subject-object relationship). The person is not subordinate to the Buddha, nor is nature subordinate to the person.

Everything, without exception, is dominant over everything else
and at the same time subordinate to everything else. This is com-
plete emancipation and freedom from any kind of bondage, result-
ing from discrimination.

3. Shunyata implies spontaneity or naturalness, not as a counter
concept of human agency, but as the fundamental ground for both
humanity and nature, for change in both human life and nature.
Accordingly, it is beyond any kind of will, including human will or
God's will, or the will to power in Nietzsche's sense.

4. In shunyata, there is both the interpenetration and the mutual
reversibility of all things. This is a natural consequence of the pre-
viously mentioned mutuality of dominance and subordination of
all things. The unity of opposites is fully realized in shunyata
because shunyata is boundless openness without any center or cir-
cumference.[14]

In recent years, in the West, the term "becoming empty" has been used,
in some confused ways, as a synonym for "becoming enlightened" or
"attaining enlightenment," and somehow the idea of having an "experience
of emptiness" has become fashionable as a code word for "enlightenment."
Abe wisely points out that,

First, shunyata should not be understood as the goal or end of
Buddhist life, but as the point of departure from which Buddhist
life and activity can properly begin. Shunyata as the goal of
Buddhist life is shunyata conceived outside of one's self-existence,
which is not true shunyata. Secondly, shunyata is fundamentally
non-shunyata, that is, it is shunyata under erasure (shunyata).
That is the true and ultimate shunyata. This means that the true
shunyata empties itself as well as everything else. Through its self-
emptying it makes everything exist as it is and work as it does.
Shunyata can better be understood as a verb rather than a noun,
because it a pure and dynamic function of all-emptying.[15]

Both teachings of dependent-arising and shunyata are an invitation to explore the naive misunderstanding we have of the nature of our own existence and the world around us. This misunderstanding causes us untold anguish by leading us to live and make investment in things as if they are stable, permanent, and their ownership is possible by a "me" who is also a stable, permanent entity. This investment—emotional, psychological, societal—in things that follow the inexorable cycle of arising/enduring /decaying/dissolving is the primary causal factor of our anguish. The teachings of dependent-arising and shunyata are the Buddha's attempt to lead us out of the anguish. Far from being a nihilistic engagement, ending of the tyranny of mental constructs is the liberation project in Buddha's teachings.

≪ 2. The Tao of Trust in Mind ≫

THE TRANSPLANTING of Buddhism into China is one of those puzzling events that have left historians scrambling for categories of description. Some have commented that it would have been less astonishing if the Roman Empire had converted *en masse* to an imported Hinduism. Others have tried to find patterns in details. The Chinese have always seen themselves as the center of the universe. The "Middle Kingdom" is a celestial framework for the Chinese, and in their way of thinking everything of value was already known to the Chinese; they didn't have to borrow anything from anyone; their knowledge was superior to all non-Han people, who were "barbarians." For a religion to have come from the barbarian kingdoms of Central Asia and presume to teach the Han people a new way of being was a preposterous claim. Mention has already been made of the controversial essay by Hu Shih, a scholar whom Arthur Wright, a more objective historian of Chinese Buddhism, includes among those Confucian historians "who regarded Buddhism as an alien cultural excrescence, and the Buddhist periods of Chinese history as shameful chapters in the life of a great people."[16]

From the very beginning, therefore, an attempt was made to sinicise Buddhism. Arthur Wright calls the years 65–317 C.E. "the period of preparation" in the sense of preparing Chinese culture to receive foreign ideas. A legend grew that Shakyamuni Buddha was actually Laozi (Lao-Tzu), the legendary founder of Taoism, who had decided to be reborn in India and teach the barbarians there. Thus, in this legend, what was coming back to China was in fact a teaching of Laozi and therefore acceptable. Other historians have argued that a yoga tradition traveled orally from India to China about 1000 B.C.E., but the Chinese, in adopting it, wholly recast its wisdom into their own form and purpose and then articulated it in Laozi's *Daodejing*.

When an alien worldview enters a culture, the degree to which it is favorably received has perhaps less to do with the worldview itself than with the internal conditions within the culture that the worldview is entering. A contemporary commentator has astutely noted:

> All times are out of joint, but some are more out of joint than others. Like ours. Like Chuang's. China of the fourth century B.C.E. bears such a strong resemblance to our own time that it brings to mind Santayana's comment that if we do not learn the lessons of history we must relive them. It was a time of ever-accelerating material progress.[17]

But it was also a time of the Three Warring States, a period of much chaos and carnage.

> Chuang [Tzu]...spoke for a generation weary of hearing about benevolence and righteousness [of the Confucian ideology] in the midst of slaughter. He advocated a return to simplicity in order to regain individuality. He rejected the mass behavior of man the bad animal, and urged a rediscovery of spontaneity. He believed that the only enduring discipline was self-discipline. All that contained the possibility of good, all that was constructive, and all that was evolutionary, was summed up in the phrase, "the attainment of the Tao."[18]

The Tao by definition had always been there, its principle implicit in the *I Ching*, one of the touchpoints of Chinese civilization. But Zhuangzi (Chuang Tzu) made it explicit at a time when the country was drowning in political upheavals and senseless carnage. His writings were the first explicit challenge to Confucian orthodoxy (Laozi's *Daodejing* had remained in the background more as a benevolent counterpart to Confucian classics) and established a certain pattern that was to allow Buddhist ideas to creep into the Chinese framework later on. This pattern highlighted the fact that any condition of political anarchy undermined the Confucian claim of providing an ideal template of social and political stability. It was in these periods of cultural self-doubt about the viability of Confucian ideology that first Taoist and then Buddhist ideas found a foothold in China.

The period 220–589 C.E.—between the downfall of the Han and the establishment of the Sui—was another such period of travail and disunity in Chinese history, and it was in this period that Buddhist ideas got a favorable hearing as an extension of Taoist ideas. Of course, over more than two millennia, Confucian ideologues found ways of co-opting both the Taoist and Buddhist ideas. The nature of Chinese culture is essentially syncretic and pluralistic. And it is this inclination toward synthesis that allowed Buddho-Taoism to emerge in East Asia in later centuries. But even before Chan emerged in China as a discernible movement, the Taoists were teaching the superiority of intuitive thought over rational rigidity that mocked the Confucian assumptions about life and society. The Taoist notion that intuitive insight surpasses rational analysis found a strong echo in the Prajnaparamita sutras of Indian Mahayana, and it is said that "when Taoist naturalism met Indian Mahayana metaphysics, the result was Chan."[19]

In this sense, Zhuangzi must be considered one of the ancestors of Chan.

> His way was one that pointed and permeated; it did not invade or seek to control. In Chuang's pages we feel the conviction that only the self-discovered truth is the truth that can be lived. His Ultimate was a course, a cosmic force. So Chuang talked of this Tao, this road, this way of life—this spontaneity that cannot be captured, only fostered; this It that cannot be labeled because it has no name.[20]

This early Taoism of Laozi and Zhuangzi was a philosophy, not the religion it later developed into—a distinction roughly equivalent to the difference between the life of Jesus and the religion of the Catholic Church; or perhaps even the difference between the early mendicant community of the Buddha and his disciples and the institutionalized Buddhism that later developed into the countries of Asia as forms of State Buddhism.

> Chuang was that chameleon of the Warring States period who was part psychologist, part philosopher, part mystic, and part Hippie. That he laughed and played the clown is evidence of his humanity. More easily, with his cocked wit, he could have derided and humiliated. But he never wearied of talking with seekers—not even those who spoke the daily recitative of cliché. He never tired of

pointing the general direction—in a rough way. Without loss of patience he told it over and over again as he saw it; but obliquely.

He was, of course, driven into the idiom of the absurd. When one has expanded his consciousness—call it *satori, samadhi,* enlightenment or mastery of the Tao—one's thought enters the paraverbal. Then to communicate with others who have not yet crossed that bar requires parable, metaphor, satire, or nonsense. The absurd becomes that third point to which both consciousnesses can relate, and through which ideas can be exchanged. Indirection is then seen as guidance.[21]

If this Taoism was anarchy, it was utterly benign, without personal ambition, or nihilism. It offered a soothing contrast to the political and social anarchy that was all around. Chuang's rebellion against the conditions of his own time are not unlike the musings of the *shramana* culture of the Buddha's time. The shramanas rejected the claims and pretensions of the Brahminic ideology of their time much as the Taoists rejected the claims and pretensions of Confucian ideology in Chuang's time.

Much as this similarity between Taoist and Buddhist/Chan ideas might be heartening, the acceptance of Buddhist ideas in China took several centuries and tensions were far from easily resolved. India and China were (and are) very distinct societies with worldviews that are essentially at odds with each other. Historians such as Arthur Wright and Kenneth Chen have pointed out these essential incompatibilities between the Indian and the Chinese mind, and the problems of "translation" from one culture to another. Among these difficulties we find that:

1. Chinese philosophers were intensely interested in the problems of this mundane life; by contrast, Indian philosophers were concerned primarily with the problems of the mind and spirit, such as the nature of the supreme impersonal creator of the universe.
2. Chinese thinkers were primarily interested in how to improve human relations; how to make their social institutions work without strife; how to create a just and enduring political system. By contrast, Indian religious thinking had stratified the entire society into four castes (the priests, warriors, merchants, and serfs) and the outcastes; political institutions were not supposed to tinker with this structure of the society.

3. Chinese society was characterized by a remarkable degree of social mobility; by ability and by conquest a bandit could become the founder of a new dynasty, and the head of an imperial family; by education a son of the soil could rise to become the chief minister of the land. In India, the social mobility was extremely limited; the Brahmin-priests were keepers of esoteric knowledge, custodians of any educational system; the warrior class only ruled through their sanction; the outcastes could never be anything else.

4. For the Chinese, existence was very pragmatic; their world was very much limited by what they experienced in the present life. By contrast, Indian thinkers, in their metaphysical speculations, peopled the universe with countless world-systems; they extended the life duration of an individual through successive rebirths; they created heavens and hells that the earth-bound Chinese never dreamed about. The Indian mind is essentially otherworldly and does not share the pragmatism of the Chinese.

5. For the Chinese, time and space is finite, oriented toward this lifetime and the generations (ancestors) that have just preceded this lifetime; for the Indian mind, the conception of time and space is infinite and aeon-oriented.

6. For the Chinese, family and secular power are supreme; the Confucian ideology provides the framework in which both live in a mutually benevolent relationship. Their social contract is predicated on the pursuit of the good society. For the Indian society, there was no social contract outside the caste system between the secular power and the individual or the family.

7. For the Chinese, individual and societal goodness meant that all able-bodied men and women should marry and beget children; they should engage in some kind of work, which would produce goods for others to use and to enjoy. For the Indian religious tradition, quest for the wisdom uniting man with the creator, or the supreme wisdom that is beyond duality was the highest purpose of man; celibacy and mendicancy were proclaimed the highest ideals of life.

8. Chinese philosophers were not inclined to analyze the personality into its components, whereas in India a highly developed science of psychological analysis existed both within and outside Buddhist tradition. The Abhidharma compendium is one of the great achievements of this science of psychological analysis.

9. For the Chinese, this life is something good and is to be lived to the utmost; for Indian thinkers, life was characterized by misery and suffering, and the purpose of life was to escape from it.

10. For the Chinese the universe has not only an origin but also has a center; for Indian thinkers, the world has no origin and no center.

These are broad cultural categories, no doubt, but there is every reason to believe that among highly specialized thinkers in both cultures there must have been kindred spirits who were able and willing to differentiate their differences and find a common thread. Certainly the acceptance of principles of Mahayana Buddhism is a case in point. Kenneth Chen, the historian of Chinese Buddhism, has remarked that the presentation of Mahayana Buddhism (with its Bodhisattva model) as a "religion of love and compassion and oneness of mankind taught by the Buddha served as a bridge between these two cultures for about a thousand years."[22]

It was indeed the Mahayana ethic of universal salvation that was appealing to the Chinese. While the pursuit of spiritual power and nonsocial goals was self-evident in India, in China it could be accepted only when it "benefited" the society. A natural outcome of this tendency was the demand and presence of the "miracle worker" in Chinese Buddhism. It can be argued that despite the modality in early Chan of praising the equanimous mind in its primary texts such as *Trust in Mind*, the miracle-worker developments were what sustained Buddhism in the life of Chinese people over centuries and generations.

Even more than worldviews and ideas about society and cosmos, the barriers of language were formidable indeed. For the Chinese, thinking about things means painting a picture and seeing it as a vision.

Further, Chinese philosophers regard language as essentially social, and language is used as a means of expressing oneself socially. Written Chinese language, being ideographic rather than alphabetic, is ambiguous and full of multiple interpretive possibilities. The educated person gained the ability to make distinctions through writing skills and sort out the discrepancies that arose frequently due to tonal pronunciations (such as the differences between spoken Mandarin and Cantonese). Furthermore, the ability to discriminate is also a learned, socially defined skill that means a person's education reflected the key skill of picking one of several meanings of a single word appropriate to social situation and setting at the time. The use of a

word in a verbal construction could obscure or illuminate the underlying
meaning of the speaker. This is somewhat similar to the sophisticated use of
double-entendre in the English language.

Such pragmatic use of language made it more situation-specific rather
than completely embedded in a theory of meaning, concepts, beliefs, or
ideas. The contrast between Chinese and Western language theories (includ-
ing Sanskrit) was that the Indo-European languages arose as an interaction
between reason and the world. The Chinese language, on the other hand,
developed as an interaction between the observer's *perception* and the world.
When Buddhism came to China, especially in the years before the great
Buddhist translator Kumarajiva (who lived in the third and the fourth cen-
turies), the Chinese transposed their language system onto Buddhist ideas.
In trying to understand Buddhism, the Chinese philosophers were not look-
ing for meaning or beliefs or ideas; these could be supplied by the existing
system of Chinese thinking. What intrigued them was the presentation of
the Buddha as a cosmic figure who would rouse himself from deep trance to
deliver discourses (namely, the sutras) to human beings. This kind of cos-
mic figure had not existed in Chinese thinking and they were intrigued by
the possibilities this image presented. They tried to fit this picture into the
picture already present in their own system.

Chinese language is "uninflected, ideographic, and (in its written form)
largely monosyllabic; [with] no systematized grammar." Whereas Indo-
European languages are "highly inflected, alphabetic, polysyllabic, with a
highly elaborated formal grammar." Further, the resulting literary modes
for the Chinese were "terseness, metaphors from familiar nature, limited
imaginative range, concreteness"; whereas in Indian Buddhism these modes
represented, "discursiveness, hyperbolic metaphor, unlimited imaginative
flights, predilection for the abstract."[23]

Whatever other drawbacks there might have been in the translation of
Buddhist teachings from Indian languages into Chinese, the terseness, the
concreteness, and the use of metaphors from nature provided Chan monks
a vehicle to convert an already existing template from Taoist sources into
songs of enlightenment of their own, celebrating a heady mixture of empti-
ness and suchness unfolding in the world of nature all around them at all
times. Nothing could be more different than the often grim, puritanical
approach of Indian Buddhists but as we noted earlier in Edward Conze's
observation, "Nothing could look more different from a tadpole than a frog

and yet they are stages of the same animal, and evolve continuously from each other."

As mentioned earlier, the modality of "miracle worker" is the dominating theme of Buddhism in China (as opposed to, say, the analytical, scholar-monk paradigm in India), and therefore it is not surprising that the earliest modality of Buddhism coming into China is as a religion of magic and mystery. The cult of Guanyin (Kwan-yin, or, in Sanskrit, Avalokiteshvara, the bodhisattva of compassion) dominates folk medieval Chinese Buddhism almost to the exclusion of other forms of Buddhist thought and practice. The Pure Land tradition became a religion of the masses in China whereas it is only hinted at in the Indian tradition—the Pure Land seems mostly a metaphor in most of Indian Mahayana sutras. Creation of cosmological spaces is very much a trend in Chinese traditions and the creation of numerous Pure Lands by buddhas and bodhisattvas fit very nicely into the Chinese framework.

Despite differences in language and worldviews about society and individuals, Buddhist teachings were carried into China on the back of the legend that Laozi had chosen to be reborn as Shakyamuni Buddha in India in order to teach the barbarians. It was therefore quite natural for the Chinese to fit Buddhist ideas and teachings into an existing system of Taoist and Confucian terms. The result was to lose the specificity and precision of Indian Buddhist languages, and make them more permeable in Chinese usage. This endeavor was given the name of *ko-yi*, "matching concepts," or interpretation by analogy.

Tao, for example, was used as an interchangeable term for Dharma. The Tao is "empty," "deep," "silent," and "complete"; it is the mother of the universe; the same attributes are applicable to "Dharma" in Chinese Buddhism. *Wu-wei* (nonaction) was used interchangeably for nirvana; *Chen-jen* (immortals) was used to denote arahants, the saints of Indian Buddhism, to make them fit into the existing Taoist cosmological framework even though that framework was totally alien to the Indian Buddhist tradition.

The term *wu*—"not" or "nothing" (familiar in the case of Zhaozhou's famous dog)—was used for shunyata with somewhat more agreeable results. While *wu* may not have had the linguistic precision of, say, the Madhyamika usage of *shunyata* as a synonym for dependent-arising, it does become a useful tool in the negative use of language to convey the underlying positive experience. Shunyata is a reconfigured awareness, and *wu* also underscores the value system of a reconfigured awareness in the Taoist tradition. The phrase *wu-wei* is one of the core units of the Taoist value system and it contains within it a spirit that was to become crucial to Chan tradition. Alan Watts writes that:

> Among the several meanings of *wei* are "to be, to do, to make, to practice, to act out"; and in [other contexts] it means "false, simulated, counterfeit." But in the context of Taoist writings it quite clearly means "forcing, meddling, and artifice"—in other words, trying to act against the grain of *li*. Thus *wu-wei* as "not forcing" is what we mean by going with the grain, rolling with the punch, swimming with the current, trimming the sail to the wind, taking the tide at its flood, and stooping to conquer... *Wu-wei* is thus the lifestyle of one who follows the Tao, and must be understood primarily as a form of intelligence—that is, of knowing the principles, structures, and trends of human and natural affairs so well that one uses the least amount of energy in dealing with them. But this intelligence is, as we have seen, not simply intellectual; it is also the "unconscious" intelligence of the whole organism and, in particular, the innate wisdom of the nervous system. *Wu-wei* is a combination of this wisdom with taking the line of least resistance in all one's actions. It is not the mere avoidance of effort.[24]

Properly speaking, then, *wu-wei* is a conduct rather than inaction, and means that actions are performed with a sensibility that reveals a care and respect for things unfolding in their natural ways. A conflation of *wu-wei* with *upaya*, skillful means, seemed a natural fit for the Chinese understanding of the bodhisattva model. Neither *wu-wei* nor *upaya* is guided by an imposition of personal preferences over any given situation because the self-referentiality has been so transcended that in one there is a total commitment to not forcing anything beyond its natural contours, and in the other, a total commitment to the welfare of the other.

Beyond the linguistic mishaps, there were certain similarities between Taoism and Buddhism. Both shared worship without animal sacrifice; both placed emphasis upon concentration, breath control, abstinence from certain foods, and a life of self-discipline. Both advocated control of passions, avoidance of luxury, purity of action and thought.

In China there has always been a syncretistic tendency, a willingness to harmonize different ideas and ways of being. Thus the "three religions of China"—Confucianism, Taoism, and Buddhism—could coexist perhaps uneasily but largely amiably for a almost 1500 years. The Chinese collectively recognized that each had a different strength and these strengths could be harmonized to work effectively in the lives of human beings.

> Buddhism, like all Indian religions, is primarily concerned with the individual rather than with the community;... [the sangha] is not a 'church' of which the laity form the mass and the clergy the elite; much less is it a community of all the faithful bound together by simple beliefs and ritual practices as Islam.... It is the community of the 'elect,' and the elect have never been more than a tiny minority of those who call themselves Buddhists.
>
> [By contrast] Confucianism...is the religion of an ordered society.... It is a religion that looks back to a golden age when all things were supposed to have been held in a balance of perfect harmony, man himself co-operating effortlessly and spontaneously with the powers of Heaven and Earth, with which he formed a coequal triad. Taoism looks back even beyond this to a time when what it calls the Great Unity was still unbroken, and man lived in a perfect harmony with birds and beast, perfectly content because he had not yet learnt to differentiate. He had not learnt to differentiate between life and death, right and wrong, pleasure and pain, profit and loss: he was still perfect and whole because his life was merged in an uninterrupted flow of all natural things.[25]

The Taoist argument locates itself in what it considers to be the pristine state of consciousness: when there was consciousness but no self-consciousness. Today's brain science calls this state a function or property of the limbic part of the brain, the one we humans share with the animals. For the Taoists this lack of self-consciousness was synonymous with the pristine simplicity of the Tao in which all mutability and change can take place without the reactivity of self-consciousness.

Thus even before Sengcan wrote his poem, and even before Bodhidharma arrived in China, a ground had been prepared in which Taoist and Buddhist ideas collaborated with each other, mainly in opposition to Confucian ideas, and found a healthy respect for each other. In times of political stress, when Confucian ideology was temporarily discarded, the Buddho-Taoist synthesis could be given a new flavor. The synthesis had the virtue of appeasing the Confucian hardliners by posturing that it was largely Chinese rather than a wholly alien system of thought from India.

Kenneth Chen argues that

> As a result of the vicissitudes which followed in the wake of the breakdown of Han imperial authority, scholars and literati who normally sought and found service in the governmental bureaucracy no longer had such opportunities for officialdom open to them, and so they turned away from practical politics and human events to take refuge in poetry, wine, and the quietism of non-activity of Taoism. Because of this, they were sometimes called Neo-Taoists. In this quietistic atmosphere of Taoism they found consolation and solace in a fundamental idea which the Taoists developed, that of *tzu-jan* (naturalness or spontaneity). In the realm of human activities naturalness was associated with the full freedom of the individual to act and talk as he pleased, unrestrained by the conventions of society. In the realm of nature it was pointed out that although no one did anything, everything was produced continually and naturally. In this sense naturalness was equated with no-activity.[26]

The real issue here is the human tendency to try to control the outcome of things according to our preference. In nature, things manifest themselves according to a complex networking of causes and conditions. The activities of squirrels lead to the planting of an oak tree, and the activities of bees pollinate the flowers so fruit can grow, but this is all done without any attempt on any one's part to "manifest" an oak tree or a flower. The squirrel and the bee are acting naturally according to their squirrel-*ness* or bee-*ness*. Buddhist teachings on karma also place emphasis on understanding the dynamic of causes and conditions rather than behaving as if our karmic history is of no consequence.

"Buddho-Taoism," then, is a collaboration of these neo-Taoist philosophers and Chinese Mahayana Buddhist monks, both of the scholarly and the ascetic persuasion. The two traditions of Mahayana Buddhism and Taoism stand in contrast to Western philosophical traditions, which have well-defined terms,the subject matter subdivided, and built up into a connected whole. The function of Taoism and Mahayana Buddhism is to offer a "big picture" worldview of the human condition into which details are fitted to complete the picture. Western scientific philosophy, on the other hand, focuses on verifiable facts and clear definitions. The contrast, then, is between vision and facts, between demonstration and analysis. The "demonstration" is obtained in a personal experience that is subjective but nonetheless convincing for people going through similar experience. Philosophy in China, in this respect, is not very different from the art of poetry; it interprets what is, instead of describing it objectively. Laozi had looked at the way (tao) things manifest themselves in nature in harmony with their natural causes and conditions (an apple seed sprouts an apple tree and a chestnut seed sprouts a chestnut tree), and he proposed that this also is the way (Tao) human beings should take. The ideal then is the person who behaves in accordance with the nature of things rather than willfully trying to change or subvert things. Each situation has its own ethic and if one moves according to the ethic of the situation, one is a person of Tao.

Laozi's philosophy is based on experience, not on any religious tradition, but mythological elements are incorporated in it that have male or female characteristics.

The new language of Buddho-Taoism that found its most creative expression in Chan is based on a certain distrust of linear, analytical language. This new language was not concerned with establishing a Truth in an abstract way; its emphasis is on the experiential, and its purpose is to bring the experience of this moment in line with the workings of nature; the Tao of nature is the Tao of man, and vice versa.

This new language discarded the old rigid system in which personal experience must fit into an impersonal truth; it insists rather that any claim of an impersonal truth must be tested against each of our own experiences. The ideal in Buddho-Taoism, then, is more that of the sage who asks, "How should I live my life?" than that of the Buddhist philosopher who might be interested in abstract knowledge. "Knowing" and "Being" are one seamless piece for the Buddho-Taoist sage; "Meaning" is to be found within the unfolding of experience rather than outside of it.

This new language and its implicit new ways of knowing and being both captured the inherent teachings of Laozi and Zhuangzi and articulated

Buddhist ideals of freedom in a creative new enterprise.

> [Zhuangzi] advocated a non-directed method of participation in nature, a Way of learning the course of things, of developing a capacity to allow things to happen spontaneously, a living of life from one's subtle, inward guidance. Chuang saw many schools and many theories but one basic problem: moral choice.[27]

While Chan's "attaining the way" (seeing into one's own Buddha-nature; insight into the emptiness of phenomena; transcending the separateness of self) was psychologically and linguistically compatible with the core teachings of Laozi and Zhuangzi ("the attainment of the Tao"), its ideal of living in mountain community settings was also close to native Taoist models. Partly because Chan generally did not contravene the teachings of native Chinese ideas, it became and remained the most prominent of the Chinese religions for many centuries. Princes and peddlers became willing students of Zen and in their own way embraced its simple, Taoist-like, lifestyle. The appeal of Buddho-Taoism moved effortlessly into different strata of Chinese society; and by about 750, as Chan, it had moved beyond its simple roots to become the pursuit of poets and emperors.

⊰ 3. The Chan of Trust in Mind ⊱

THE ARRIVAL OF BODHIDHARMA, the legendary Indian founder of Chinese Chan, is one of those seminal events in Chinese Buddhist history whose significance, even as legend, cannot be overemphasized. It has become the foundational block for Chan's mythologizing of itself in later generations. Bodhidharma is reputed to have been a Buddhist monk from a princely family in south India who appeared at the court of Emperor Wu in the present-day city of Nanjing in 520 C.E. The legends of Bodhidharma, Huike, and Sengcan are generally taken at face value as historically true by Zen adherents in East Asia, but there is only fragmentary mention of these personages in early Chan records. Indeed, many scholars have suggested that Chan "retrofitted" its own ancestral history (given the peculiar Chinese emphasis on ancestor-worship and its transposition on issues of lineage and legitimacy within religious communities) when it needed to do so in the eighth and ninth centuries, and used the fragmentary mentions to claim them as its patriarchs.

The received tradition of Chan is, however, so firmly rooted in Bodhidharma's legend that a brief mention helps us see the context of Sengcan's poem for later generations. It is said that when Bodhidharma appeared at the imperial court (for the one and only time), the emperor, who was a devout Buddhist, enumerated for him how many temples he had had built, how many monks and nuns he had supported, and how many sutras he had had copied with his own hands. "What," he then asked the bearded monk, "is the merit of all this great work?"

"None whatsoever, your majesty," replied Bodhidharma without missing a beat!

This is perhaps the only account in Chinese Buddhism of an emperor-patron receiving such an uncompromising reply to his supposedly holy works. It is not surprising that in a highly stratified society such as the Chinese, this became for later Chan monks a model for telling things as they are, without pulling any punches. Puzzled, the emperor asked Bodhidharma, "What is the central teaching of Buddhism?" to which the monk replied, "Vast emptiness, nothing holy." This again was not a reply the emperor was familiar with, or could accept or even understand. Finally, the frustrated patron asked the monk, "Who are you?" (meaning what are your qualifications to give me such crazy answers), to which Bodhidharma is said to have nonchalantly replied, "I have no idea."

The literal translation of Bodhidharma's response is, "This is not-knowing" but its deeper meaning gains currency and a certain panache in the more vernacular phrasing of "I have no idea" or "Don't know." Regardless, the use of the phrase "Not-knowing" connects Bodhidharma instantly to the existing Taoist notion of *wu-nien* (no thought), and is one of our first glimpses into a specific Buddho-Taoist vocabulary in the history of Chan.

The legend of Bodhidharma goes on to say that he and the emperor did not become great friends after all, and Bodhidharma crossed the mighty Yangzi river to travel north to the Shao-lin temple where he meditated in a cave for nine years. It was during this period that Huike, the future second ancestor, appeared outside the cave and asked for teaching. Bodhidharma continued to ignore him for days even after it snowed and Huike stood outside the cave knee-deep in snow. Finally, according to legend, he cut off his arm and threw it in front of the meditating monk. This seems to have caught Bodhidharma's interest, and he finally asked him, for all practical purposes, what was his problem, why was he going to such extreme lengths to get Bodhidharma's interest.

In the Dharma encounter that followed, Huike narrated how he had been trained as a Confucian scholar and read all the classics, and yet his "mind was not at rest" and he implored the master to bring it to rest. To this, Bodhidharma demanded brusquely, "Give me your mind and I will put it at rest for you." Huike was dumbfounded for a long time and said finally, "When I look for my mind I cannot find it." Instantly, Bodhidharma declared, "There, I have pacified it for you." The legend of Huike tells us that as soon as he heard these words, he came to a profound awakening.

Sengcan's own encounter with Huike a generation later sounds quite like Huike's interview with Bodhidharma. If imitation is the best form of flattery, a suspiciously large number of Zen encounters between teacher and student follow this pattern of Bodhidharma-Huike encounter. In an oral culture, succeeding generations were no doubt grateful for this stylized imitative privileging. Bodhidharma is said to have left behind a poem that has since become the basic building block of Chan inspiration:

> A special transmission outside the sutras;
> Without depending on words and letters;
> Pointing directly to one's own mind;
> Seeing into one's true nature and realizing Buddhahood.

Whatever the historical uncertainties of Bodhidharma's legend, there is a nice symmetry between the sentiments of this poem and Taoist ideas. To this symmetry Sengcan brings his own unique voice and creates a synthesis that becomes a touchpoint for generations of practitioners in the so-called golden age of Chan in China (roughly 750–1050 C.E.). R. H. Blyth is of the opinion that,

> It was the inner meaning of these Four Statements [of Bodhidharma] that Sengcan desired to perpetuate in the five hundred and eighty four characters of this poem. In it he has condensed the essence of all the Buddhist sutras, all the one thousand seven hundred koans of Zen.[28]

At the same time, Bodhidharma's poem and his replies to the emperor were not without their Chinese Buddhist context. Sengchao (circa 374–415), the brilliant but short-lived disciple of Kumarajiva (the great Central Asian monk who had rendered accurate translations of Buddhist sutras from Sanskrit into Chinese for the first time in Chinese history; active in China 401–411 C.E.) had already attempted an interpretation of Buddhist wisdom (*prajna*) through the Taoist lens of "unknowing." Sengchao wrote,

> A thing called up by a name may not appear as what it is expected to appear; a name calling up a thing may not lead to the real thing. Therefore the realm of Truth is beyond the noise of verbal teaching. How can it then be made the subject of discussion? Still I cannot remain silent.[29]

Sengchao was a Taoist who saw Nagarjuna's work (translated by Kumara-jiva from Sanskrit into Chinese in 409) as an extension of the writings of Laozi and Zhuangzi. In the surviving writings of Sengchao there is a dis-trust of words, and an unmistakable preference for immediate, intuitive knowledge, both of which were to be hallmarks of Buddho-Taoism as it emerged in subsequent centuries, and as it had been developing embryoni-cally in centuries prior to Sengchao. He was at ease with the paradoxes cre-ated by wordplay that leaves the meaning ambiguous but points to the truth that lies behind words. This truth had to be experienced, not reasoned out. His biographer declares "Sengchao interpreted Mahayana; [the Chan founders] Huineng and Shenhui rethought it."[30]

Another historian of Zen says,

> The relationship of Sengchao to Zen is to be found in his orienta-tion toward the immediate and experiential perception of absolute truth, and reveals itself in his preference for the paradox as the means of expressing the inexpressible.[31]

Daosheng (ca. 360–434) was another brilliant student of Kumarajiva who is often credited with advancing the idea of "sudden enlightenment" that became a hallmark of later Chan. He is said to have remarked,

> The symbol is to express an idea and is to be discarded when the idea is understood. Words are to explain thoughts and ought to be silenced when the thoughts are already absorbed.... It is only those who can grasp the fish and discard the fishing net that are qualified to seek the truth.[32]

One historian has remarked that, in saying this, Daosheng "identified the Taoist idea of wu-wei or 'non-action' with the intuitive, spontaneous appre-hension of truth without logic, opening the door for the Chan mainstay of 'no-mind' as a way to the ultimate truth."[33]

The great genius of Chan in China was to move from any abstract debate about "form and emptiness," as has been the case with Buddhist philosophers ever since the two terms were conjoined first in the *Prajnaparamita Hridaya* "Heart Sutra." Chan located itself, by contrast, in the pragmatic, existential mode of "form and function" while taking the inherent emptiness of *all* forms for granted as its background. Equating emptiness with, and facilitating its movement toward, "function" became a truly revolutionary stance in Chinese Buddhism. It allowed the mature Chan tradition to fulfill the promise of the bodhisattva model without getting caught in the abstract philosophical debates about the premises of the model itself (viz., how can one show compassion for forms that are inherently empty?). The self-emptying of form is the truest function of shunyata, and it is only through this self-emptying (i.e., "emptying of self") that the enlightened function of the form is seen. It is imperative for the form of, say, a bodhisattva to empty itself *first* of any notion of bodhisattva in order to function as a bodhisattva. The function of the bodhisattva itself is *shunya* (empty) or tracked by *shunyata* (emptiness) because the form has self-emptied; so long as there is a trace of the form, the function is not pure shunyata. In other words, in order to function as a bodhisattva, one must transcend the duality of self (consciousness) and form ("the other").

The poem *Trust in Mind* speaks primarily of the functional aspect of form/being in the world when it speaks of emptiness. We don't know whether or not Huineng (638–713), the sixth ancestor of Chan, active about a hundred years after Sengcan, was familiar with the poem, but he was the first to articulate the sentiments of the poem in the doctrinal formulation of "Meditation is the substance of wisdom; wisdom is the function of meditation; they are like the flame and the lamp."[34] This was a completely new way of looking at meditation as form (the lamp) and wisdom as emptiness (the flame),for which there is no comparable language in Indian Buddhism.

Huineng reasserted the territory that was first explored by Sengchao, and later articulated by Sengcan. In Huineng's Platform Sutra (the foundational text for the "new" Chan— the "old" Chan was, definitionally, the Chan of Bodhidharma and was identified the with Lankavatara Sutra as the primary text), we find the fullest crossover yet of basic Chan and Taoist ideas: the ordinary mind of man is deluded, and the practice of no-mind *(wu-shin)* is considered sufficient for the rectification of that deluded mind. Closely allied to *wu-hsin* (no-mind) is *wu-nien* (no-thought), and when combined with *wu-wei* (nondoing or non-action), we have, within the literature of "new" Chan, a full-fledged collaboration with Taoist ideas.

Even before Sengcan or Huineng, the Taoists had proposed that no-mind or no-thought is not a nihilistic state but a conscious cultivation of a nondual or non-discriminating mind. In no-mind all dualities or distinctions are let go. Positively stated, this no-mind is One Mind because it is nondual. This Taoist notion is the basic building block of the *Xinxinming*.

Ultimately *Trust in Mind*, like the *Daodejing*, is about how to be a sage. In it we find the first explicit statement of how a Chan sage was going to be different from earlier understandings in China of a Buddhist sage. These understandings were based on the Indian Mahayana ideal of the bodhisattva, as articulated in Prajnaparamita sutras. Huiyuan (344–416), founder of the Amitabha Pure Land school and a contemporary of Kumarajiva, had become the model of a holy person for succeeding generations of Chinese Buddhists. But he was a transitional figure, working in an environment where the core ideas of Indian Buddhism were still being understood through Confucian and other cultural terms. Kumarajiva and his translation bureau had done monumental work in rendering accurate translations of Buddhist sutras for the first time in Chinese during the last years of Huiyuan's life, but it would take several generations for this accuracy to filter down. Even during Sengcan's own lifetime, more than a hundred and fifty years after Kumarajiva, the founders of the new schools of Tiantai and Huayan were struggling with a structural ordering of the massive doctrinal material they had inherited from Indian Buddhism.

During Sengcan's lifetime Chinese Buddhism was in the midst of great intellectual ferment in addressing the nature of mind. A central figure in this enterprise was the Indian missionary monk Paramartha (499–569) who arrived in Nanjing in 546 at the court of Emperor Wu of Liang dynasty. This was only twenty-six years after Bodhidharma had arrived at the same court, and whose "interview" with the emperor was presumably still the talk of the town. Unlike Bodhidharma, however, Paramartha was a translator (he ranks in Chinese Buddhist history at the level of Kumarajiva and Xuanzang, the famous translator of Yogachara texts—a very elite company indeed). He was not an iconoclast like Bodhidharma, and his reception seems to have gone much more smoothly.

> At the time of Paramartha's arrival in China in 546, even though Buddhism had permeated intellectual thought, institutions, and the arts in both north and south China, Indian sutras and shastras were still regarded as dogma that could not be tampered with, and intentional innovations in Buddhist philosophy by the Chinese were rare.[35]

But it's reasonable to assume that the bomb that Bodhidharma threw into Chinese Buddhism still had a lit fuse. For one thing, it seems to have introduced *dhyana*, or meditation practice, into elite Chinese Buddhism that up until that time had been more enamored of scholarly and intellectual pursuits. It seems equally reasonable to assume that the effects of Bodhidharma's bomb were working their way among the communities of ascetics and hermits, both Taoist and Buddhist, who would, in coming generations, become the standard-bearers of the emergent Buddho-Taoism.

This new movement seems to have existed parallel to the creation of great philosophical systems compatible with Chinese culture and imagination in the Sui and Tang dynasties (late sixth to mid-ninth centuries). These included the schools of Huayan and Tiantai both of which

> ...developed on the basis of Paramartha's translations and as a response to his She-lun (Xelun) school. Their principal masters, Chih-I (Zhiyi) of T'ien-t'ai (Tiantai) school and Fa-tsang (Fazang) of Hua-yen (Huayan) school had thoroughly studied Paramartha's main works, and these texts inspired their creation of systematic and distinctly Chinese versions of the ideas that Paramartha transmitted. Chan Buddhism, too, used Paramartha's corpus as a foundation for its attempts to reform Buddhism during the T'ang (Tang) dynasty.[36]

Some scholars have argued that Sengcan's poem may have also been influenced by the teachings of the Huayan school.[37] It seems a tenuous argument, at best. Although the school was not fully systematized until Fazang (643–712), its beginnings have been attributed to Dushun (557–640), now recognized as its first patriarch. Dushun is a younger contemporary of Sengcan and it's hard to see a broad enough circulation of Dushun's ideas during Sengcan's lifetime to impact his insights.

In short, there were many changes in Chinese Buddhism during Sengcan's lifetime. Both the philosophical and the meditative explorations were trying to engage with the nature of mind in new creative ways. Paramartha himself was a scholar-monk of the Yogachara school that in India had displaced the early Abhidharmic approach to mind within the Mahayana thought. This new understanding flirted with substantializing or pseudo-substantializing interchangeable terms like *shunyata, Buddha-nature,*

Mind, Buddha-mind, and so on. This new understanding was influencing the newly emergent dhyana or meditation communities (of which Sengcan was a part) and how they influenced Sengcan's own understanding of One Mind. The pseudo-substantialization of One Mind or Buddha-mind (or nirvana) has been an ongoing ontological problem for Buddhist practitioners since very early days. The Buddha had refused to propose an ontology (he was a phenomenologist) precisely because he rejected the substantialist ontology of the atman or Brahman that the Brahmanical philosophers of his day were proposing. But the seduction of the "ultimate" is a powerful force in the human mind, and Buddhist philosophers throughout were pressured to define an "ultimate" in Buddhist teachings. Hence, periodic correctives like Nagarjuna's dialectic and Chan's deconstructive use of language to protect against the temptations of substantialism.

And yet when we speak of Chan in China, we need to keep in mind that we are speaking of a thousand experiments on a thousand mountain peaks. There's the official history that claims an unbroken lineage through Bodhidharma, the twenty-eighth ancestor, and going back to Shakyamuni Buddha himself, but there are different cultural realignments (or shifts or movements) in almost every generation of Chan that challenge the monolithic and monochromatic claims of the official history.

In brief, the key points are these:

1. The first movement in Chan is from Bodhidharma to Sengcan when Chan monks—most likely few enough to be counted on the fingers of both hands—lived the ascetic life of wandering monks and perhaps begged for their food, much like the shramanas of Buddha's own time.
2. The second movement is from Daoxin (Tao-shin) to Hongren (Hung-jen), the fourth and the fifth ancestors, where Chan monks were living in large monasteries supported by wealthy local patrons, and following institutional structures.
3. The third movement is of Huineng, the sixth ancestor, who established a farming community as a new model for Chan monks without critical dependence on patronage from local warlords or merchants.
4. The fourth movement is of Shenhui, the combative disciple of Huineng, who came close to establishing Chan as a state religion under the patronage of Empress Wu.

5. The fifth movement is the wild, iconoclastic Zen of Mazu Daoyi (Ma-tzu Tao-i), the inventor of shock tactics—the crazy wisdom approach. This was the era of mountain monks living in small communities away from prolonged interactions with society down below in the plains.
6. The sixth movement is the organization of "monastic rules" under Baizhang (Pai-chang) Huaihai, the renowned disciple of Mazu.

Several shifts or movements later is the adoption of Chan as a house religion by Sung emperors in the tenth and eleventh centuries. What we find in Japan and Korea today are mostly the remnants, to varying degrees, of the Chan that functioned as a state religion in Sung China. In Korea, until recently, there was a living tradition of the Chan of the Tang period where mountain monks in isolated communities supported themselves through meager farming in the less than ideal fields around the "temple." The larger and more impressive monastic complexes of Korea and Japan are a testimony of the time when rulers in these countries called themselves Buddhist and subsidized the building of ever larger temples as part of an imperialized Buddhism.

As a model of Buddhist practice, the life and teachings of Sengcan puts him much closer to wandering *shramana*-monks of Buddha's early communities and to Zhuangzi than to a state-sponsored Chan.

With Mazu (709-788) and his eighty-six successors, there is a whole new language and way of speaking that is as much Taoist as it is Buddhist. This new Chan consciously separates itself from the "old" Chan of Bodhidharma and his successors. At least on one level, the old Chan was based on the legend of transmission from master to disciple through handing over Bodhidharma's robe and bowl, and his copy of the Lankavatara Sutra. In the new Chan, the transmission is "mind-to-mind" and it does away with any symbols of institutional or scriptural affiliation.

This "mind-to-mind" transmission became a postmodern modality in medieval China long before twentieth-century philosophers discovered postmodernism. In this transmission everything is experiential and experimental rather than scriptural or institutional. There is only the encounter of one mind with another in present moment, and the context of that encounter is established right then and there. If the encounter takes place in a boundless openness without any assumption or agenda, then the encounter is authentic. Within the authenticity of the encounter there's no investment in its outcome. (As a historical footnote, this creative "post-modern"—in the sense of a rigorous process-orientation rather than goal-orientation—transmission of early Chan became a formalized lineage transmission in medieval Japanese Zen in more rigid, and more institutional, ways than it ever did in the Chan and *Son* traditions of China and Korea.)

The language of Sengcan's poem is the first evidence we have of the creation of a new style of language in Chinese Buddhism that departs from the baroque, flowery language of Indian Mahayana sutras, and is very influenced by Taoist sentiments. This was at a time when early masters of Tiantai and Huayan schools were still translating and using the baroque, flowery language of the Lotus Sutra and Avatamsaka Sutra respectively, into Chinese. Sengcan and the fledgling tradition of Chan were not interested in establishing a "Truth"-with-a-capital-*T* but rather in finding a template for living with awareness and clarity. In that sense, they were expressing the original message of the Buddha. The goal of the mature Chan tradition is not to answer questions but to dissolve the lust for or addiction to seeking answers and to diminish suffering thereby. In our complex conditioning, we pose metaphysical questions in a way that we are seeking to confirm an answer that we wish to have (e.g., Does God exist?). Despite our protestations, what we are doing is not a search for truth but a solace for our conditioned existence. It is true, as the saying goes, that the truth shall set you free but what's generally not said is that before it sets you free it will destroy you (or rather, your conditioning). For the Buddha, this shattering of conditioning is tantamount to freedom. And very few people want to experience this shattering. Chan practitioners sought to get out of this shell game.

When we work through two-and-a-half millennia of accretions we find that the Buddha himself was not interested in any revelatory "Truth." Chan was a rebellion against the kind of institutionalization and scripturalization that tended to obscure this original message of the Buddha.

When Sengcan's poem and other Chan texts are using the language of traditional Buddhism, they are placing themselves within the doctrinal context of Mahayana Buddhism; when they are using the language of paradox, it is to place themselves within the free-wheeling tradition of Zhuangzi's Taoism. In the mature tradition of Chan we find a creative synthesis of two basic Indian Mahayana ideas of shunyata and upaya coupled with the Taoist hermitic notion that "chopping wood and carrying water" are the most "miraculous" of activities (when these activities are done nondualistically).

The teaching of upaya or skillful means is the arch that connects the Prajnaparamita tradition of Indian Buddhism with Chan in China. The basic premise of the teaching of upaya is that once *drishti* (vision, view, theory, perspective) has been purified and converted into *prajna* (transcendental wisdom), all that is left to do is to live directly in the world rather than through concepts. And living in the world means "functioning" in the world. Functioning in the world is either skillful or unskillful (in the sense of being harmful or beneficial to oneself, others, and the world). In both Chan and bodhisattva models of Indian Mahayana, there is an understanding of upaya as both "function" (as verb) and "functioning" (as noun)....This understanding of upaya as "function-in-functioning" parallels our earlier discussion of bhava as "Being-in-becoming." There is no "function" in any abstract sense outside of "functioning" just as there is no "Being" in any abstract sense outside of "becoming"; there is just the encounter with things of the world in their "suchness" (just as they are) and our response/function in that encounter. The crying of a child is just the crying of the child without any metaphysical implications and our response to that crying determines our "being-in-becoming," either skillfully or unskillfully. A nuanced understanding of both upaya and bhava means that we are not what we think but what we do. Of course, since intention precedes action, a bodhisattvic action requires the establishment/purification of a bodhisattvic intention. In the eightfold path proposed by the Buddha as a prescriptive cure for the ills of the world, right intention *(samyaksankalpa)* flows naturally from right view *(samyakdrishti)* as we orient our heart-mind away from grasping and toward liberation for ourselves and others. Intention, in turn, is the motivation for the particular speech or bodily act that follows. This is the birthplace of karma, and this is where skillful means becomes a living, experiential action rather than an abstract idea.

One of the critical roles the teaching of upaya plays both in Indian Buddhism and in Chan is to "bridge the seeming incompatibility of emptiness and compassion. Indeed, emptiness and compassion themselves may be regarded as skillful means."[38] In the Lotus Sutra, which became a hugely influential paean in China and Japan to skillful means, this inherent incompatibility of emptiness and compassion is skillfully resolved.

A view common to all schools of Buddhism is that the Buddha's approach to teaching was primarily therapeutic, that he used a variety of strategies in assessment of the abilities of his audience to bring his listeners to a realization of nirvana. Upaya is synonymous with the view that sees all of Buddha's teachings as antidote to dukkha rather than an appropriation of a particular viewpoint as an ideology. This particular approach to the Buddha's teachings could most effectively collaborate with Taoist ideas in China and became a precursor to the emergence of Chan, which has never been an ideology or theology.

> The value of approaching the teachings of the Buddha as a relative truth, as therapeutic rather than absolutist, lies in the fact that it allows one to see all the contradictions and inconsistencies as only apparent. Teachings are appropriate to the context in which they are given; their truth is relative and so the contradiction evaporates. This is essentially a non-dogmatic approach to truth where one is investigating one's own experience with complete honesty.[39]

I have written elsewhere that it may not be an exaggeration to say that Mahayana is a history of upaya in search of buddhas,[40] and when Sengcan writes his poem as a cure for the ills of the world, he is offering the upaya-therapy of how not to cling to things. In this upaya-therapy, everything is seen as provisional and relative, a play of shadows against the background of shunyata.

There's a very simple core to the Mahayana argument of shunyata that's now being confirmed by research in quantum physics: that there's no such thing as "Reality" in an absolute sense; what we have instead is a provisional reality within the confines of time and space. The logic of these findings suggests that if everything, bar none, is a provisional reality, all the tools and technology to understand that reality are also provisional. This argument suggests further that all iconic representations including the buddhas, Zen teachers, lamas, arahants are all provisional representations. What follows further in this argument is that the participant too is a provisional reality participating in a provisional reality of which s/he herself is a part and always has been, but s/he is not aware of this original nonseparation of his/her own provisional reality from the provisional reality all around.

This argument does not mitigate the need for an effort to search for an undeluded recognition of provisional reality as such, as well as a behavior based on skillful means within the provisional reality. The Avatamsaka Sutra equates upaya with nonclinging, thus aligning the heart of Buddha's teachings with skillful means (as post-non-clinging engagement in the world). If everything is provisional, one does not need to cling to a reified sense of reality because in its provisionality, all things have the nature of anitya (impermanence) and anatman (non-substantiality).

In their provisionality, all things are undifferentiated from each other (due to lack of a core substantiality), and do not admit the dualism or separation of subject and object. This nonduality is the "suchness" *(tathata)* of things. In their provisionality, things are just as they are, without any transcendent core privileging their provisional appearance. Provisionality/non-differentiation/suchness is immanent in all things as the equalizing core of all provisional appearances. It is critical that this suchness be experienced rather than be privileged as a theory. In suchness, the primacy of experience comes either through intense meditation experience or some other breakthrough in perception. It is equally critical that such an experience be cognized (through the wisdom of shunyata) as highlighting the provisional, undifferentiating, nonprivileging nature of all things. Without this cognition, it's all too easy to fall back into old habits and longings, and recapitulate the core empty nature of all things as representation of something abiding.

The suchness/*tathata* of Mahayana Buddhism resembles the *holos* or "holographic whole" of quantum physics. In the boundless openness of the *holos* there is a nondifferentiation and nonseparation between the whole and its parts. The whole is as much a process as are individual parts. None exists as an object-in-itself, or subject-in-itself. When things are not seen as objects-in-themselves and are seen only processes, being empty of an abiding core, suchness becomes synonymous with function which, in its positive aspect, is skillful means. In its negative aspect, function is synonymous with delusions *(avidya)*—clinging to views and things as objects-in-themselves.

In his inimitable way, Edward Conze has this to say about *upaya*:

> "Skill in means" is the ability to bring out the spiritual potentialities of different people, by statements or actions which are adjusted to their needs and adapted to their capacity for comprehension. If the truth be told, all that we have described so far as constituting the doctrine of the Mahayana is just "skill in means" and nothing more. It is a series of fictions elaborated to further the salvation of

beings. In actual fact there are no Buddhas, no Bodhisattvas,
no perfections, and no stages. All these are products of our
imagination, just expedients, concessions to the needs of
ignorant people., designed to ferry them across to the
Beyond. Everything apart from the One, also called
"Emptiness" or "suchness," is devoid of real existence,
and whatever may be said about it is ultimately untrue,
false and nugatory. But nevertheless it is not only permis-
sible, but even useful to say it, because the salvation of
beings demands it.[41]

The line above, *"Everything apart from the One, also called 'Emptiness' or 'such-
ness' is devoid of real existence, and whatever may be said about it is ultimately
untrue, false and nugatory,"* sums up the central themes in *Trust in Mind*, which
alternately uses "oneness" and "suchness" as correlates for emptiness in
much the same way as Conze does. Neither Conze nor Sengcan would priv-
ilege "One" as a substantialist doctrine. They avoid getting into a monothe-
istic trap by equating it with shunyata. Shunyata as suchness obviates a
nihilistic as well as a substantialist ideology as discussed earlier.

Much more than in the language of Indian Mahayana, suchness *(tathata)*
became one of the core teachings of Chan in China, and its conflation with
shunyata allowed a new sensibility to emerge that is positive and yet consis-
tent with the logic of emptiness. (This conflation is present in some of the
Indian Mahayana Prajnaparamita sutras, such as the "Diamond Sutra but the
sensibility is little different.) As the discussion in Appendix I makes clear,
experiments in quantum physics have shown that at their core all phenom-
ena are undifferentiated energy. Even though each phenomenon may mani-
fest itself as wave or particle, the core energy remains indivisible. In shunyata
teaching, all things, without exception, are empty of own-being and there-
fore, in an absolute sense, have complete equality. This complete equality is
suchness. Any attempt to discriminate or privilege between this and that is
a denial of this underlying equality. In its suchness (manifested) aspect, each
thing is complete as it manifests itself (whether as wave or particle); in its
shunyata aspect, each thing is emptying itself out to return to a state that is
before wave or particle. In this equation, suchness is the manifest; shunyata
is the unmanifest. They are synonyms, and it is in this synonymy that they
were used by Sengcan and other Chan teachers.

A restatement of the basic idea of Heart Sutra—"Form [suchness] does not differ from emptiness [shunyata]. Emptiness does not differ from form. That which is form is emptiness; that which is emptiness form," a conflation of suchness (as form-in-emptiness) with *bhava* (being-in-becoming) and *upaya* (function-in-functioning)—should provide a basic understanding of how Indian Buddhist ideas were configured in China, and how they speak to the historical context of *Trust in Mind*. The inner logic of this synthesis suggests that:

1. All phenomena are empty at their core (shunyata).
2. Each phenomenon is in a state of suchness *(tathata)*; they each have the same nature, are completely equal, and one cannot be privileged over the other.
3. Therefore, the only thing that's relevant are skillful responses *(upaya)* in each situation rather than a value system based on a conceptual framework.

Although Sengcan's poem does not speak directly of this creative synthesis, this is how the mature tradition of Chan came to engage itself with the empty world: through skillful means in mundane activities of life rather than a doctrinal rigidity.

To sum up, when the traditions of Buddha's teachings, Taoist naturalism, and Chan come together in *Trust in Mind* as three intimately interlinked strands, we find a shared commonality of perceiving the self and the world in a certain way.

This shared commonality sees that:

1. "Self" and "things" are processes and are characterized by an ever-changing coreless open-endedness.
2. "Reality" is not substance but a network of causal happenings that create different manifestations in each moment.
3. Hence the issue is existential, not ontological.
4. The deeper issue is our distorted perception of self and the world.
5. Liberation is cleansing the lens of perception, not accumulation of speculative views.
6. Language itself has only a conditional value and its meaning is always tied to the context in which it appears.

Sengcan's poem is a compact but potent articulation of these commonalities in a language that is immediate, graceful, and elegant.

❧ Part Two ❧

≼ Commentary ≽

HISTORICAL BACKGROUND

Xinxinming is a poem of 146 lines of four words each (a total of 584 characters in Chinese), and is written in Chinese almost without any Pali or Sanskrit words. Stan Lombardo, one of the contemporary translators of the poem, has this to say about the structure of the poem:

> The expression in the poem is very concise, even for Chinese, and the concision imparts a certain kind of directness and force. The poem is in the form of 146 lines, each consisting of four characters, that is, four monosyllabic words or phrases, rather than the longer and more typical lines of Chinese verse consisting of five or seven characters each. The lines do not rhyme, which adds to the plainness of expression. The Chinese text is written in vertical columns, without any indication of grouping of lines into stanzas, but it is obvious that the lines are composed as couplets; that is, each line is a complete clause, but a sentence consists of two lines.
>
> Further, couplets usually can be paired to form quatrains, four line stanzas. But these quatrains are not fixed, discrete units. The logical progression of the poem is such that the last two lines of a given quatrain could as well be the first two lines of the next, creating an interlocked tension in the movement of the poem. In any case, since there are 146 lines and 146 is not divisible by four, the couplet is clearly the basic unit of thought. The main point here is that a translation should reflect the original poem's style and structure, which are not simply esthetic features but essential to the meaning of the text.[42]

Xinxinming is our first example of a purely Chinese Buddhist text without overt references to Indian Buddhist tradition (these references, as we have seen in the first part, are implicit). The poem, or its origin at least, is attributed with fair certainty to Sengcan (whose name means "Jewel of the Sangha") whose probable dates are circa 526–606 C.E., and whom the historical tradition of Chan considers its third ancestor. There is very little information about him and what we know about him comes from stray references here and there in early Chan texts. He is said to have come to the second ancestor, Huike, at the age of forty when he was still a layman and suffered from leprosy.

As noted earlier, his first encounter with Huike is suspiciously reminiscent of Huike's own first encounter with Bodhidharma, and thus may not necessarily be a historical fact.

One of the legends that has come down to us is that after Sengcan practiced with the second ancestor, he was cured of his leprosy. He is also said to have gone into hiding along with other monks during the persecution of Buddhism in 574. Where his community was, or how many monks were in it is unknown. Most likely it was a peripatetic community of monks who probably begged for their food from local villagers. The only verifiable date in Sengcan's legend is the year 592 when the fourteen-year-old Daoxin (ca. 578–651), the future fourth ancestor of Chan, became his student. This legend says also that after he shared his last meal with other monks, Sengcan stood up and grasped the branch of a tree nearby, and quietly standing there he died. (The probability of this legend can go only so far as it incorporates the symbolism recurring throughout various Buddhist legends of Queen Mayadevi giving birth to the Buddha while standing up and holding the branches of two trees.) The year is said to have been 606.

The only other record of Sengcan's teaching available to us is from the stone tablet at his memorial. It says,

> Simultaneously practice stillness and illumination. Carefully observe, but see no dharmas, see no body, and see no mind. For the mind is nameless, the body is empty, and the dharmas are a dream. There is nothing to be attained, no enlightenment to be experienced. This is called liberation.[43]

THE TITLE

The title of the poem, when written in Roman characters using the Pinyin system of transliteration, is "Xinxinming." In the Wade-Giles system it is "Hsin Hsin Ming" (as has been done by numerous translators), or alternatively "Hsin Shin Ming." Yet any transliteration leads to some difficulty especially as the Wade-Giles system has been commonly used for the last one hundred years or so. Even though they sound very similar, *hsin* and *shin* are two different characters. *Hsin* is represented by a person standing upright, while the character for *shin* represents the heart (or, in Chinese understanding, the heart-mind. The Chinese have never made a sharp distinction between the psychological and the emotional; throughout all Buddhist literature, when one is talking about "mind," one is talking about the total package of the psycho-emotional network). The common translation for *hsin*, the first character, is "faith" or "trust" (trust in someone who is standing upright, or who stands by his/her word); for *shin*, the second character, the common translation is heart-mind.

When using the Wade-Giles system, writing the two words as *hsin* ("faith" or "trust") *shin* ("mind") seems to provide greater clarity. The Japanese phonetic phrase *Shinjinmei* ("The Song of Faith and Mind") provides equal clarity when breaking it down into a Japanese/Chinese/English comparative sequence: *shin/shin*/mind; *jin/hsin*/faith; *mei/ming*/song.

We should also note that in Chinese there is no distinction between a noun and a verb; thus *hsin* can mean "trust" or "trusting" or "to trust." *Ming* is usually translated as "verse" but can also mean a "written expression," "warning," or "admonition." Thus another translation of the title could be, "Admonition on the Trusting Mind." The title has also been variously translated as, "Inscribed on the Believing Mind" (D. T. Suzuki); "On Trust in the Heart" (Arthur Waley); "Trusting in Mind" (Stanley Lombardo); and so on.

Needless to say, the "faith" in the title is used not in a Christian sense of faith in something outside of oneself, but in the sense of a trusting mind; and the trust is in what has been directly experienced, in direct knowledge (*prajna*), and a conviction coming out of that experience and knowledge. This is represented in the ideogram as the person standing upright, with self-assurance. I have chosen to use the translation "Trust" rather than "Faith" to avoid the otherwise inevitable difficulties of context in a Judeo-Christian understanding.

LINE-BY-LINE COMMENTARY

The Great Way is not difficult for those who have no [addiction to] preferences:

The first line of the poem is a classical Taoist formulation and many modern readers find in this one line a source of constant renewal and rededication to practice. The Chinese (and East Asian generally) literary and social protocols do not emphasize the personal pronoun "I" and often when a statement is made about a seemingly universal truth, it really is an expression of a specific personal experience. Consequently, one has to wonder whether there is an autobiographical note in this first line. Is it possible to see Sengcan's poem as a "song of realization," articulating a place of deep inner experience, in much the same way that Hindu mystics, Tibetan Buddhist saints, or Amazonian shamans have expressed themselves after their own breakthrough experience?

Perhaps, this line might indicate that the Great Way has not been difficult for him (Sengcan) personally and therefore all people can have the same (not difficult) experience. Or perhaps Sengcan is emphasizing only a deep personal experience and not a teaching in the traditional sense, there being no "others" to be taught. All of this fits into the general spirit of Zen and Buddhist teachings.

The Buddha did not claim any divine revelation in the hour of his enlightenment but is said to have proclaimed that he had only "rediscovered" an ancient truth. The power of his teachings came from the premise that anyone else can discover the same truth if the required effort is there. In other words, the Great Way is open to each and every one of us, and every person is capable of becoming a buddha. But the Great Way is not simply information that we can assimilate while munching on a doughnut. Its realization requires effort over a long period of time and its premise is nothing less than a total, radical transformation of our perceptual processes.

In the Zen tradition, when the word *practice* is used, it does not always refer to formal training. The "training" itself is done in the zendo (meditation hall) but "practice" is done at all times of the day. Training is formal discipline but practice is mindfulness in all moments of daily living. At some point the two merge to create a discipline of life, a discipline of the habits of body and mind and heart. This is the Path, the Great Way, and it is fully embodied—not an abstract metaphysical concept.

In conventional usage, both *Path* and *Way* indicate there is a "road" to be traveled; there's a sense of a journey to be undertaken; there's a sense that this journeying has been done by others before us and that the path is well-trodden. There are markers on this path and if one is willing to travel on this road with courage and discipline, these markers will facilitate the journey. There is an implication that the path leads to a place of ease and restfulness.

The eightfold path of the Buddha has more of a specified structure, in keeping with the analytical approach of the Indian mind, whereas the Great Way of Buddho-Taoism seemingly has no structure—and yet both are in the service of an ease of being in the world.

A contemporary scholar has made an interesting observation on the relationship of the Tao and the Buddhist Path:

> It is first of all essential that we appreciate the rich polysemy of the term "tao." In general, the term functions both as a noun—in the sense of a path, a way, a manner, a method, and as a verb—in the sense of blazing a trail, proceeding in a certain way. In Chinese Buddhism, Tao is also used to denote both the Buddhist Path or Way (Sanskrit: *marga*) and the fruit resulting from its practice. That is, Tao connotes both the Noble Eightfold Path and the enlightenment which it allows to be realized.[44]

I have added the qualifier "addiction to" (preferences) in my translation of this first line to point to a richer and deeper meaning of the poetics of the original phrase. It takes us into an understanding that the real issue is not the mere fact of the preferences themselves. We make hundreds of preferential choices in our daily life and they are neutral in and of themselves. But when we find ourselves willing to defend those preferential choices at the cost of our deeper experience we are stepping into the realm of addiction.

In the Pali tradition, the word for happiness is *sukkha* but when we unpack the word, there is nothing really graspable about it. In a deeper sense of the word, sukkha is the *absence* of dukkha, an absence of stress, of anguish. It is the result not of appropriation but of letting go. And letting go is the letting go of our preferences, or, more precisely, letting go of our unconscious addiction to our preferences. This letting go is letting things be without

wishing them to mold themselves around our preferences. Ajahn Chah, one
of the great forest monks of the last century in Thailand, says,

> Try to be mindful, and let things take their natural course. Then
> your mind will become still in any surroundings like a clear forest
> pool. All kinds of wonderful, rare animals will come to drink at
> the pool, and you will clearly see the nature of all things. You will
> see many strange and wonderful things come and go, but you will
> be still. This is the happiness of the Buddha.[45]

In translating this first line of the poem, various translators vacillate
between "preference" and "pick and choose." Here are some examples:

"The Perfect Way knows no difficulties
Except that it refuses to make preference."   (Suzuki)
"The Perfect Way is only difficult
for those who pick and choose."   (Waley)
"Attaining the Way is not difficult
Just avoid picking and choosing."   (Sheng-yen)
"The Great Way is not difficult,
Just have no preferences."   (Lombardo)
"The Great Way is effortless
for those who live in choiceless awareness."   (Dunn and Jourdan)

It may be that the sense of the original Chinese is much closer to our con-
temporary term "preference" even when the literal words are "pick and
choose." To translate "pick and choose" as "choiceless awareness," as Dunn
and Jourdan have done, is a bit of linguistic stretch, but as a poetic genre it
conveys a much deeper sense of the intention of the poet. It certainly offers
a glimpse into the meditation-as-mindfulness trajectories of the later Chan
tradition, and it may be a somewhat more helpful term for the practitioner.
Of course, in recent times, "choiceless awareness" has been made an integral
part of any discussion of spirituality by the teachings of J. Krishnamurti, the
great philosopher-mystic from India. This term also finds corroboration in
the practice of *shikantaza*, the "just sitting" practice of the Soto Zen tradi-
tion; the zazen of shikantaza invites choiceless awareness of the breath, and
discourages any preference for one manifestation of breath over the other.

When love [likes] and hate [dislikes] are both absent, everything becomes clear and undisguised:

In classical Buddhist formulation, the basic causes of dukkha or anguish are greed, hatred, and delusion. Greed *(lobha)* is the factor of wanting to grasp on to and hold things or experiences we like or love; hatred *(dvesha)* or aversion is the other extreme of wanting to push away things or experiences we dislike.

When we closely examine our own personal world of preferences, of picking and choosing this over the other, we find we are essentially trapped in a world of reactivity, pulled this way and that in response to what we like or don't like. But, through meditation, we can cultivate a way of being in which this reactivity is absent, and then it is as if we are looking at things directly rather than through a distorting lens. Sengcan tells us clearly: completely let go of all conditioned reactivity, live through non-reactivity, and each moment will be a new perceptual unit in which we can act freely and appropriately.

In the English language, *love* and *hate* are perhaps too strong to accurately capture the sensibility of the poem. This sensibility is more about likes and dislikes, which is the translation used by Waley, Lu, and Lombardo. The contemporary reader might find it useful to substitute like/dislike for love/hate, respectively, in this line.

The conditioned self has built up, through processes of appropriation and projection, an intricate construct that is its self-identity and also its filter of perception of the phenomenal world. In each moment of interacting with any new data, both of these constructs, based on an underlying series of likes and dislikes, come into play, and our perception of reality becomes distorted. These constructs are the filters of delusion or misperception.

When the nature of the self and the nature of phenomena are both understood to be informed by shunyata, there is gradual erosion of existing edifice of constructs as well as a slow-down of new construct-making. We begin to chip away at this edifice by cleansing the lens of perception to see how the cycle of longing, clinging, and becoming is working in our life to cause dukkha. This is a long, painful process, and is not likely to happen overnight. But its effect is to gradually build up a sense of equanimity *(upeksha)* that provides a counterweight to the reactivity of likes and dislikes. In those moments when likes and dislikes have been truly replaced by equanimity, "everything becomes clear and undisguised"—revealed to be empty of own-being *(svabhava)*. From this perspective, we are aware of the space between the primary point of direct apprehension of the lack of own-being in things and the secondary moment of their appropriation. We are aware of our freedom to *not* appropriate any experience, to not fit it into our conditioned matrix of likes and dislikes, to not make a story out of it.

Sengcan's admonition about "love" being absent pushes us into uncharted territory since we have been so conditioned to believe that "life" is all about "love." We may be willing, even eager, to let go of hatred, but the idea of letting go of love evokes a different response. Why? When we examine both of these categories of experience very closely, we find that at the core of each one of them there is an energy struggling to manifest itself. Like the wave-particle equation of quantum energy, it can manifest itself as either hate or love depending on what conditions are present to facilitate that particular manifestation. Psychologists tell us that love and hatred are directly related. Yet Buddhist teachings tell us that the energy underneath both of them is neutral and it is only the presence or absence of mindfulness that will determine whether the energy manifests in a wholesome or unwholesome way. Our continued investigation will reveal that each one of these categories is a projection of our own needs—psychological and emotional—but there is nothing or no one at the other end except these projections meeting the restless energy in an echo chamber. When Sengcan is talking about love and hate being absent, he is really talking about the absence of all these psychological, emotional, and conceptual projections, and even about the absence of attachment to these projections. Our challenge is to not become attached to any of these projections.

In Taoist sensibility, absence of likes and dislikes means an embrace of all things rather than a rejection of all things:

> To embrace all things means first that one holds no anger or resistance toward any idea or thing, living or dead, formed or formless.
>   Acceptance is the very essence of the Tao.
>   To embrace all things means also that one rids oneself of any concept of separation: male and female, self and other, life and death.
>   Division is contrary to the nature of the Tao.
>   Forgoing antagonism and separation, one enters into the harmonious oneness of all things.[46]

Make the smallest distinction, however, and heaven and earth are set infinitely apart:

Remaining trapped in the world of preferences we are led to an expectation of how things *should* be. When our expectation of how things should be conflicts with how things are, there is dukkha. *(anguish)*

In our likes and dislikes, we want to control things, and in that preference to control things, "heaven" and "earth" get separated. In Chinese linguistic usages, "heaven" and "earth" are metaphors for the "higher" (whatever that may be in Chinese understanding) realm and the realm of the mundane, earthly life. For the Chinese, the purpose of existence is to create a harmony between these two realms (even though in reality there is only one realm). "Heaven" and "earth" are also metaphors for all opposing dualities that create tension, stress, ill-will, for the individual as well as society at large. In the poem here, "heaven" and "earth" point to certain mind-states: a sense of ease or a sense of dis-ease. When we are at ease, we feel light and free and bouncy; when we are not at ease, we feel heavy, dark, and limited. Sometimes we may feel one way and sometimes the other—and our likes and dislikes come into play causing us to grasp onto one and shun the other. Equanimity provides the sense of ease that becomes available only after likes and dislikes have been brought to a complete rest. Any time we make distinctions based on our addictive preferences, there is a lack of harmony, a lack of balance, a sense of incompleteness in our experience of this moment. Sengcan says "heaven and earth are set infinitely apart"; in the vernacular of our time and place we might say "something is off."

Huineng taught that meditation is the "substance" of wisdom, and wisdom is the "function" of meditation. Similarly, clear seeing becomes the "substance" of equanimity. Clear seeing is seeing the self and the world from inside out through the framework of shunyata; clear seeing is the corrective lens of perception in which delusion has been wiped away, at least momentarily.

Dunn and Jourdan translate this line poetically and succinctly (if rather freely) as, "Even the slightest preference, and your whole world becomes deluded."

If you wish to see the truth, then hold no opinions for or against anything:

Having likes and dislikes necessarily means holding opinions for or against the object of our like and dislike. In turn these opinions cloud the lens of perception and our vision of things becomes distorted and disfigured. We never see the truth of the object of perception in this state; rather we always see the object through a series of filters based on our preferences, our likes and dislikes, the conditioned opinions we hold for or against the object.

Certain wise teachers have pointed out that despite all the claims to the contrary, most human beings don't really wish to see things as they really are, because this truth is threatening to one's cherished structure of beliefs, a threat to the likes and dislikes that we have worked so hard to put in place and through which we gain our sense of identity. We only want to affirm our pre-existing ideas or prejudices about things, not deconstruct them. This is part of the root cause of dukkha, our sense of anguish and alienation. It is always there underneath like a well-spring, whether we are consciously aware of it or not.

The line, "If you wish to see the truth" can serve to expose any pretensions to "spirituality," any desire for feel-good solutions that don't require having to give up, often painfully, the construct of self-identity.

water ▷ A metaphor for holding no opinions for or against anything is water poured from one container to another. Water offers no resistance whether it is poured into a square pan or a round bowl, into a tall slim vase or a fat bottle. It moves effortlessly in meeting the requirements of the "container" but never ceasing to be water.

A word of caution is in order here, I think. The injunction for not holding any opinion for or against relates to issues of self-identity and self-reification; it does not serve to marginalize the issue of personal and societal ethics. The entire framework of the Buddha's teachings depends upon *shila*, personal ethics, and both *samadhi* (meditation) and *prajna* (wisdom) are ultimately in the service of this personal ethics. The wisdom of not holding any opinions liberates us from constant self-referencing but there is a larger understanding of what's harmful to ourselves and others. Sengcan, like all Buddhist teachers, encourages us to live this nonharming life in the service of all.

To set up what you like against what you dislike is the disease of the mind:

Ever since we started using our neocortex and its associated language-based selfing, we have carried on chatter within ourselves. The nature of the internal chatter is to proliferate itself in ever more complex ways. *Prapancha* (*papancha* in Pali) is the wonderful Buddhist word for this proliferation. It does not matter what the sources of *prapancha* are; the fact remains that proliferation keeps the engine of internal chatter going at all times. Degrees of sanity or insanity depend on the volume and intensity of the internal chatter. In the case of a person untrained in the Dharma, this internal chatter, especially when chattering about "what I like" or "what I don't like," is the "disease of the mind."

The internal chatter creates a feedback loop in which selfing feeds upon itself and creates an ever-more complex proliferation, like a virus infecting all parts of the system.

Buddhist meditative traditions have found ways of transcending the internal chatter and clarifying those aspects of mind/wisdom that have not been infected by the disease of internal chatter. When we transcend the internal chatter we enter "silence"; the heart-mind becomes illuminated by the inherent wisdom of the mind itself. This silence/wisdom does not make distinctions, does not dwell in dualities of this or that, for or against, and yet is aware of itself as a purified state. This awareness is not subject-object relationship, or verbal, or ideological, for any verbalization or conceptualization is part of the internal chatter and, eventually, self-defeating.

When the deep meaning of things is not understood, the mind's essential peace [stillness] is disturbed to no avail:

The deep meaning of things is that things have no own-being *(svabhava).* The working of the internal chatter is driven by unexamined beliefs that things have their own self-sustaining "reality," their own validation. We become invested in things, whether psychological or material, because we believe, at least implicitly, that things—and our apprehension of them— are real. What we rarely understand is that we apprehend only our *idea* of things rather than things themselves. Selfing drives the engine of internal chatter, disturbing the original stillness of the mind, and leaving the problems of

dukkha still unaddressed. All the training in meditative traditions is geared
to somehow stop the noxious internal chatter that prevents mind from illu-
minating itself.

Sheng-yen translates the word "essential" as "mysterious principle" but
it is mysterious only in the sense that the stillness of the mind does not lend
itself easily to verbal descriptions. It is a primordial experience, which is just
barely described by the word "stillness." As soon as it is objectified, we lose
its essence. We can "be still" and only then have a taste of the original still-
ness of the mind that's there underneath all distorted perceptions.

The deep meaning of things is seen through the framework of shunyata.
The purpose of the shunyata dialectic is to break down the fixations we have
with the nature of things as self-abiding. This is not a negation of the exis-
tence of things in a provisional sense, but only our fixations with them that
continue to disturb endlessly the stillness of the mind, and do not allow us
to enter into silence.

Lombardo translates this line as "If you miss the deep meaning, stilling
your thoughts is of no use"—which opens up the possibility of reading this
line as a relationship between meditation (stilling your thoughts) and wis-
dom (perceiving deep meaning). One of the basic critiques of the yoga tra-
dition by Buddhists in ancient and medieval India was that despite their
proficiency in concentration practices, the yoga practitioners did not under-
stand the context of original emptiness. That lack of context or deep mean-
ing of things allowed concentration practices to become yet another form
of striving. The essential stillness of mind is manifested only when all striv-
ing ceases; the ceasing of all striving itself becomes the context of a deeper
understanding of the nature of things.

The reader should note that whenever the language of "stillness" is used,
either in this commentary or in the Chan tradition, caution needs to be taken
that the intention is not to create a preference for stillness or quietude for its
own sake, but to point out that such stillness is in the service of letting go.
Letting go is an *experience* of heart-mind rather than the grip of intense inter-
nal chatter where the contents of the mind tend to get reified. This stillness
is not a trance or a yogic concentration but the equipoise in which aware-
ness is so purified that it does not make distinctions on preferential basis.

reify: to regard abstraction as real

*The Way is perfect like vast space where nothing is lacking and nothing
is in excess:*

The sources of our discontent and alienation are a sense that we are some-
how incomplete, that something is lacking. We are always striving to fill this
"lack" through accumulation of ideas, beliefs, and psychological or material
possessions. But this lack is a condition of internal chatter and when the
internal chatter is silent, there is a spaciousness that allows things to come
and go without fixating on any of them, or even their comings and goings.

Space itself is a wonderful metaphor for the Great Way. As a famous poem
puts it,

> Wild geese fly into the space,
> without leaving a footprint.

Space is neither fulfilled nor diminished by wild geese flying into it; its essen-
tial spaciousness is not disturbed and does not create conditions for the
geese's "footprints" to take hold.

When the mind is equanimous, these footprints in the shape of a sense of
lack or fulfillment do not find a foothold. This is not an idealized state or an
abstract argument but a way of being in the world that is very much within
the domain of human experience. Each one of us can experience that equa-
nimity where nothing has been completed and yet nothing remains undone.
Equanimity obviates any sense of incompleteness. The experience may even
induce a sense of completeness but we need to be very careful how we artic-
ulate that completeness; any such articulation can be a potential trap where
we bring our old bagful of wish lists.

*Indeed, it is due to our choosing to accept or reject that we do not see the true
nature of things:*

In the vast clear space, things are manifesting themselves according to causes
and conditions. The geese are flying according to the nature of geese; the
wind is blowing according to the nature of the wind; the sun is hot accord-
ing to its nature; the moon is cool according to its nature. Their manifesta-
tion does not depend on our choosing to accept or reject the nature of those

things. We get fixated in our reactivity to the blowing of the wind or the heat of the sun, and that fixation, in its self-obsession, does not allow us to see that things are unfolding according to their inherent natures. In the vast complex of networks, the manifestation of each thing depends on the underlying causal network. We can perhaps accept this intellectually but we lose our way when it is pointed out that the same is true of the contents of our own minds. Our conditioning too is a vast complex of causes and conditions and the mind-state of the present moment is but a manifestation of this underlying network. We can mistakenly identify with this mind-state as "me" or "mine" or we can just watch it come and go.

Live neither in the entanglements of outer things, nor in inner feelings of emptiness:

Sheng-yen translates this line as "Do not pursue conditioned existence; do not abide in acceptance of emptiness." The phrase "conditioned existence" speaks perhaps more precisely to what is meant by "outer things." Our conditioned existence is always reaching out and getting entangled in and seduced by whatever it comes into contact with. The hallmark of our conditioned existence is the internal chatter through which we are getting entangled with the outer world according to our own preferences—how that outer world should be or should not be. Our internal chatter, and its universe of preferences, is driven either by the thrill or excitement of new toys (grasping), or by unhappiness of one kind or another (rejecting). The new toys could be varieties of the emotional, the psychological, or the material but as more and more psychologists are seeing in the lives of children in an increasingly complex and affluent society, the factor of "boredom" kicks in much more quickly than it did in premodern, preliterate societies. The more toys there are, the less satisfaction there is in being gratified by them; conversely, whatever gratification there may be is of much shorter duration because the mind has been conditioned to getting more and diverse toys to keep itself entertained. Today we live at a hyper-speed, and our access to goods and information would be astounding to someone like Sengcan were he to see it for himself. But this very access to outer things has entangled our very lives in ways that we don't even begin to understand. Yet underneath all this access there are feelings of anguish and alienation that also seem "real" because all the access to things does not seem to address the basic feeling of lack.

Just as we can cling preferentially to external things, we can cling equally to inner feelings of alienation, or even to silence. It is important to note that genuine silence is quite different from the idea of silence. In the experience of silence, we are not looking for any particular experience but to allow the inherent spaciousness of mind to emerge in which thoughts and feelings can come and go without leaving a "footprint." A genuine silence is also a place of fullness; nothing is lacking and nothing needs to be completed. In this spaciousness, there is no need to cling to external phenomena or inner feelings of alienation. We begin to see that both are issues of selfing that continue to proliferate because of ignorance *(avidya)*.

Be serene in the oneness of things and such erroneous views will disappear by themselves:

This spaciousness restores us to a serenity that is the original condition of the mind. "Oneness" is one of those cross-over words that allows us to explore both its Buddhist and Taoist contexts. For the Taoists Oneness is the Tao, which means that in the great Tao there is no differentiation of any kind; all things find their resolution in the Tao. We are perturbed only when we are in the realms of distinctions and differentiations; once we let go we enter the Tao and find serenity.

"Oneness" is not self-identity nor is it other-identity. In Buddhist usage Oneness is the "suchness" of things. This suchness *(tathata)* is "things-as-they-are" in their present manifestation; and their present manifestation is dependently arisen without any own-being *(svabhava)*. In the perspective of suchness, we can simultaneously appreciate both the absolute nature of things (empty of own-being) and their provisional nature (momentary appearance according to causes and conditions), and thereby find serenity.

Water is always "serene" in its "waterness" regardless of the different kinds of containers it is poured into. It does not cling to any erroneous view that one container is preferred over the other.

A Taoist view is relevant here:

Those who understand the Tao delight, like cats, in just sitting and watching without any goal or result in mind. But when a cat gets tired of sitting, it gets up and goes for a walk or hunts for mice. It does not punish itself or compete with other cats in an endurance test as to how long it can remain immovable—unless there is some real reason for being still, such as catching a bird. Contemplative Taoists will happily sit with yogis and Zennists for as long as it is reasonable and comfortable, but when nature tells us that we are "pushing the river" we will get up and do something else, or even go to sleep. More than this is certainly spiritual pride.[47]

The Buddha spoke again and again about the relinquishing of *all* views, not merely some, as a necessary condition for liberation. His advice to the villagers of Kalama, in the famous Kalama Sutta, speaks eloquently to how views are acquired and their letting go:

> Do not go upon what has been acquired by repeated hearing; nor upon tradition; nor upon rumor; nor upon what is in a scripture; nor upon surmise; nor upon an axiom; nor upon specious reasoning; nor upon a bias towards a notion that has been pondered over; nor upon another's seeming ability; nor upon the consideration, "The monk is our teacher." Kalamas, when you yourselves know: "These things are bad; these things are blamable; these things are censured by the wise; undertaken and observed, these things lead to harm and ill," abandon them.[48]

The radicalism of Chan pushed this envelope even further and said that *all views are erroneous* simply by virtue of their being views in the first place. The Buddha spoke of the "right view" *(samyakdrishti)* as the first element of the eightfold path by which he meant the understanding of the four ennobling truths to shed light on the universality of unsatisfactoriness, its origin, its cessation, and the path leading to cessation. The Right View here is an invitation to explore the four ennobling truths as an experiential template in one's own mind-body system rather than a metaphysical belief in one thing or another.

In practical terms, we can work with views (such as the four ennobling truths) as working propositions but when we grasp any of them as "truth" those views become instantly erroneous. Therefore, a deconstruction of all views, bar none, is required before one steps into working with them provisionally. There is an experience of serenity or equanimity when all views are let go; conversely, if the experience is strong enough and stable enough, it will deter an emergence of any view that may try to reify itself.

When you try to stop activity to achieve passivity, your very effort fills you with activity:

The serenity in the Oneness of things is not arrived at through any particular activity; rather it is attained through *wu-wei* (no action or nondoing, not trying to control the outcome of things). Wu-wei, as one of the central ideas of Taoism, means an action or inaction that takes place spontaneously and naturally but it is the activity or inactivity of the saint in whom all traces of self-consciousness have been washed out. When there is a conscious effort to stop an activity that we find undesirable, we are actually engaging in a struggle to find the opposite which we think will act as an antidote to the situation. But of course the antidote itself is a "corrective" that we are trying to impose on an inherently unflawed situation—and it ends up filling us with more chaos. We are always trying to fix things according to our own preferences, and we are not even aware that our effort to achieve, say, happiness is itself a neurotic enterprise.

For Laozi, in his seminal Daodejing:

> Thus, the wise man deals with things through wu-wei and teaches
>   through no-words.
> The ten thousand things flourish without interruption.
> They grow by themselves, and no one possesses them. (Ch. 2)

> The Tao is constant and wu-wei, yet nothing remains undone.
>   (Ch. 37)[49]

The quality of serenity or equanimity emerges when we allow things to be just as they are in their suchness or Oneness. "Activity" and "passivity" are used here in the sense of trying to "control" things rather than letting them "flourish without interruption" as Laozi says. Control could be an attempt to control the inner or the outer world in order to achieve self-centered goals; in either case it sets us up on a merry-go-round in which only the *illusion* of control is produced. Equanimity does not deny or contradict human agency but rather provides a corrective balance to the relentless self-centeredness in which we humans are taking part all the time.

Wu-wei as "nondoing" is itself the highest form of "doing" and nondoing is not a state of being catatonic but rather a skillful choice, a condition of serenity in which one does one's best according to one's ability and the circumstances but also one has the spaciousness to allow things to unfold according to their causes and conditions. One has the wisdom to accept the results of such unfolding without any struggle.

Lombardo translates this line as, "Stop moving to become still, and the stillness will move." In other words, stillness becomes dynamic movement rather than a stagnant condition. This is also the notion of *wu-wei*. For the Taoists, the sage is not one who withdraws into the life of a hermit, but is a man of social and political achievements, although these achievements must be brought about through wu-wei "non-action" or "taking no [unnatural] action."

The Taoist idea of *wu-wei* transformed itself into the Chan idea of "no-mind." Daosheng (355–434), a major disciple of the great translator Kumarajiva, was the first person to advocate the idea of sudden enlightenment (he is also the founder of the Nirvana School of Chinese Buddhism). He identified wu-wei with intuitive, spontaneous apprehension of truth without logic, opening the door for the Chan mainstay of "no-mind" as a way to ultimate truth.

There is perhaps no better expression of *wu-wei* and no-mind (which is also the One Mind) coming together than in this celebrated poem by the lay Buddhist practitioner Pang (c. 740–808) from Tang China:

> My daily affairs are quite ordinary,
> but I am in total harmony with them.
> I don't hold on to anything, don't reject anything;
> nowhere an obstacle or conflict.
> Who cares about wealth and honor?
> Even the poorest thing shines.
> My miraculous power and spiritual activity:
> drawing water and carrying wood.

*As long as you remain in one extreme or the other, you will never
know Oneness:*

Layman Pang, in the verse cited above, is very clear that he avoids the
extreme of holding on to anything as well rejecting anything. So, for him,
there is no obstacle or conflict. He stands in the space of Oneness. Trying to
exercise control whether in the form of activity *or* passivity is an impedi-
ment to living in the serenity of Oneness. Either extreme is our idea of how
things should be; and all our ideas are essentially self-referential because
they are rooted in our preferences for this or that. "Knowing the Tao" (or
"Knowing the Oneness") is not an attempt to create an ontology to justify
our preferences but the experiential quality of being at ease, being serene,
being equanimous in all the unfolding of things. Oneness is Buddha-nature
itself; it is not anything extraneous. To be completely at ease with one's own
conditioned mind, without holding on to anything or rejecting anything, is
to know the Oneness.

The basic issue here is our habitual thinking in terms of antithetical pairs,
opposites—"good and bad," "active and passive," and so on. So long as we
try to hold on to one extreme or the other, we are in opposition to the other
extreme. This creates a formidable barrier to an understanding of the under-
lying dynamism that lies beyond antithetical thinking.

*Those who do not live in the single Way fail both in activity and passivity,
assertion and denial:*

Activity and passivity (both as conditions of reactivity), assertion and denial
(both as conditions of ignorance) are all standpoints that find their basis in
self-referential delusions. When one lives in the Tao or Oneness of things all
these standpoints become false in the sense that they ultimately prove to be
mere concepts, and collide with the experiential reality of our lives. To assert
or deny the nature of things, in one sense or another, is to fail to see the
workings of the "two truths" (in the Madhyamaka dialectic of Nagarjuna)—
the absolute and the provisional. Any assertion or denial is in the realm of the
conceptual; any attempt to control activity or passivity is in the realm of
delusion.

Nagarjuna equates emptiness with the relinquishing of all views:

> The victorious ones have said
> That emptiness is the relinquishing of all views.
> For whomever emptiness is a view,
> That one will accomplish nothing. (MK 13.8)[50]

His radical understanding of emptiness encompasses all standpoints, theories, interpretations, opinions, conceptual or verbal expressions of how things have come to be.

> According to the early tradition, views are seen as deriving from a commitment to opposite-thinking, the tendency to see things in terms of basic dichotomies of which is/is-not is the most virulent. Confusion and ignorance arise on the basis of the sedimentation of these distinctions/identifications—what in early Buddhism are referred to as samskaras, habituation impulses or dispositions (with respect to speaking, thinking, and acting).[51]

Letting go of all views means disengaging oneself from the realm of abstract, conceptual reality and stepping into the world of mind-body experience in this very moment. In such an experience, as Sengcan himself says at the end of his poem, there's no being, or non-being, in abstract, conceptual ways, nor is there a denial of anything.

To deny the reality of things is to miss their reality; to assert the emptiness of things is to miss their reality:

There is no denial or assertion in the witnessing of flowers blooming in the spring or snow covering the landscape in winter. It is only when we create categorical imperatives of "flowers" or "blooming" or "spring," and so on, and spend our time and energy in defending them do we become prisoners of ignorant thought-processes. The Madhyamaka dialectic of Nagarjuna allows us to transcend the closed feedback loop of assertion and denial by seeking a "higher third."

The Madhyamaka philosophers held that shunyata (which is equated with Dharmakaya, the ultimate reality) cannot be comprehended or expressed through a mere philosophical theory. For them, logic became a tool to go beyond denial and assertion. As we discussed earlier, in Heidegger's methodology of putting things "under erasure," we have a new tool for articulating this higher third without getting caught up in linguistic gymnastics. If we put *I* under erasure as "I" we are able to transcend the assertion of "I am" as well as "I am not" in ways that open up a new vista of liberative perspective. Even the Tao or Oneness should not become an object of assertion or denial. We can put *Tao* under erasure as "Tao" to understand it as the "higher third" to bring about a qualitative change in our understanding the experience of being in the world. No category of linguistic expression is or should be immune to this methodology of "under erasure."

The more you talk and think about it, the further astray you wander from the truth:

The evolution of language has done wonderful things for us as a species, but as Buddhist thinkers have pointed out, when we use language as the representation of reality itself we end up creating a dead-end construct for ourselves that leads to existential despair. To talk and think about the Tao in assertive or denying ways is a harmful enterprise. The truth or apprehension of the nature of things happens only when the noise of internal chatter has been brought to a complete stop. Without getting into the inner logic of linguistics itself, suffice it to say that the problem here is how the language is used by the grasping mind, not the intrinsic structure of language itself.

An example perhaps is the Cartesian paradigm of *cogito ergo sum* ("I think therefore I am") by which Descartes meant to show that the only thing he can be certain of is that he is thinking, or is a thinking-being. *Cogito ergo sum* has nothing to do with the validity or lack thereof of the contents of thinking. Many thinkers since Descartes's time have, however, used his *Cogito* to support all kinds of ontological assertions. For Sengcan and other Chan masters, an assertion of reality based on the reification of our own internal chatter is a deluded entanglement.

Stop talking and thinking, and there is nothing you will not be able to know:

Miraculous things happen when internal chatter has been brought to a com-
plete stop. As noted earlier in a quote by Ajhan Chah, "[In a mind still like a
clear forest pool] all kinds of wonderful, rare animals will come to drink at
the pool, and you will clearly see the nature of all things. You will see many
strange and wonderful things come and go, but you will be still." [52]

We can understand this teaching either metaphorically or literally. The
mind that is completely still is at rest and delighting in the taste of tran-
quillity. That's a rare and miraculous taste. In that moment of stillness, the
phenomenal and the psychological worlds reveal themselves. The contem-
porary shamanic books by Carlos Castaneda, purporting to be an anthro-
pologist's training with a Yaqui Indian shaman in Mexico, highlight this
modality of entering extraordinary realms of knowledge through com-
pletely stopping the internal chatter. Castaneda's books have been highly
controversial, but there is an uncanny resemblance between the changes in
the structure of consciousness in his method and in the practice of Zen med-
itation. Both approaches are geared to dismantling the constructs that have
been put in place by internal chatter. This transcendence, whether in the
Castaneda method or in zazen, leads to a "deeper" kind of knowing that is
intuitive and spontaneous rather than a conceptual construct. The premise
of Castaneda's writings is that a condition of inner silence allows one to
open up to transpersonal worlds.

This was also the experience of Shakyamuni Buddha in the hour of his
awakening: Nothing remained hidden for him; all the worlds of past, pres-
ent, and future became known. Without getting caught up in the shamanic
aspects of Shakyamuni Buddha's experience, the Zen tradition works on the
premise that new and extraordinary ways of knowing that emerge when a
condition of inner silence has been reached yield a direct, truer knowledge
about ourselves and the world.

*To return to the root is to find the meaning, but to pursue appearances is to miss
the source:*

This inner silence is the "root" before it was covered up and marginalized by
linguistic constructs that in turn conditioned us to accept those constructs

as reality itself. In the modern age, more than ever before, we have been try-
ing to supply meaning to life through achievement, through acquisitions,
through status and position, through goals and plans but we are hardly aware
that we are always dealing with the appearance of things rather than their
inner reality. Therefore meaning is assigned to appearances, and to appear-
ances-as-reality. A conditioned compulsion to supply "meaning" compels
us to make emotional and psychological investments in the appearance of
things, and such investments eventually lead to separations into self and
other—to opposite-thinking. These investments and pursuits may serve for
a while but eventually we find them to be hollow; they do not supply us with
what we need in order to feel whole and complete. Their failure to do so, and
in the sorrow and pain that issues from that failure, we discover that we can-
not pursue the outer appearance of things. As we have been discussing,
appearances are only provisional statements of reality; at their core they are
empty of own-being. Any investment in the provisional ignores the absolute
aspect of reality and is bound to lead to disenchantment.

This line in Sengcan's poem highlights the inner tension between the
teaching of shunyata and the teaching of compassion (karuna) in the
Buddhist tradition. Shunyata-wisdom points to the "root" of things, their
lack of own-being, yet all the teachings of Buddha and other teachers also
display compassion for all things in the world. This is a paradox that is
resolved through the simultaneous practice of wisdom and compassion, akin
to the necessarily simultaneous functioning of the two wings of a bird. This
is the basic template of the bodhisattva model of Mahayana Buddhism. A
bodhisattva is active in the world motivated by compassion for all beings
while being grounded firmly in the wisdom of shunyata or emptiness. Acts
of compassion have no "meaning" in the sense of validating anything in the
bodhisattva; acts of compassion are just acts of compassion and do not need
a reason for their justification. They become *truly* acts of compassion when
the bodhisattva is simultaneously aware that these acts of compassion in
samsara are just as empty as anything else, including the bodhisattva her-
self. Buddhist traditions, including Zen, work creatively and gloriously with
this paradox.

In his comments on the Heart Sutra, which is a deconstructive text par
excellence, my Korean Zen teacher, Seung Sahn Sunim, used to say, "Human
beings have no meaning, no reason." His Western audiences were invariably
shocked into an uncomfortable silence at this bold assertion about the

human condition for which there is no viable frame of reference in the Western intellectual or religious traditions. His point was classically Buddhist: If all things are dependently arisen according to causes and conditions, there is no "inherent" meaning in the appearance of things. This is the terrifying aspect of the wisdom of shunyata and to leave it at that would be nihilistic indeed, even if it is the "absolute" truth.

My teacher would point out further that we have a choice of turning "no meaning" into "Great Meaning" and thereby entering fully into the bodhisattva paradigm of Mahayana tradition. The compassion of the bodhisattva is for the world of appearances in which deluded beings are caught in their own trap and experiencing varieties of *dukkha*. The bodhisattva is motivated to find innumerable *upaya*, or skillful means, to address these varieties of *dukkha* but never loses sight of the ultimate truth of emptiness of own-being. The bodhisattva is never confused about the "source" of the world of appearances. Through numerous *upaya*, the bodhisattva can manifest equally numerous varieties of compassion—each appropriate to the dukkha-causing situation at hand—without ever turning compassion into yet another conceptual category.

At the moment of inner enlightenment, there is a going beyond appearance and emptiness:

The "going beyond appearance and emptiness" is the bodhisattva's "acting in the world." This acting in the world is qualitatively different from the "acting out" (as the language of contemporary psychological and behavioral theories would put it) of the average person. Before acting in the world, the bodhisattva has clarified his/her lens of perception, has understood fully the dependent arising nature of all appearances, and it is through that "moment" of inner enlightenment or inner transformation that s/he acts.

Ken Wilber, one of the leading contemporary thinkers in the field of transpersonal psychology, has given us some unique perspectives from which to examine the issue of transformation. He does so by making a critical distinction between "translation" and "transformation."

> With translation, the self is simply given a new way to think or feel about reality. The self is given a new belief—perhaps holistic

instead of atomistic, perhaps forgiveness instead of blame, per-
haps relational instead of analytic. The self then learns to translate
its world and its being in terms of this new belief or new language
or new-paradigm, and this new and enchanting translation acts, at
least temporarily, to alleviate or diminish the terror inherent in
the heart of the separate self.... This function of religion does not
usually or necessarily change the level of consciousness in a per-
son; it does not deliver radical transformation. Nor does it deliver
a shattering liberation from the separate self altogether. Rather, it
consoles the self, fortifies the self, defends the self, promotes the
self.[53]

By contrast, radical transformation

...does not fortify the separate self, but utterly shatters it—not
consolation but devastation, not entrenchment but emptiness, not
complacency but explosion, not comfort but revolution—in
short, not a conventional bolstering of consciousness but a radi-
cal transmutation and transformation at the deepest seat of con-
sciousness itself.[54]

Moreover...

Transformative spirituality does not seek to bolster or legitimate
any present worldview at all, but rather to provide true authen-
ticity by shattering what the world takes as legitimate. Legitimate
consciousness is sanctioned by the consensus, adopted by the herd
mentality, embraced by the culture and the counterculture both,
promoted by the separate self as the way to make sense of the
world.[55]

For Sengcan, this radical transformation is "going beyond" the provi-
sional world of appearances and any nihilistic sense of emptiness. Both are
end-results of a sense of separate self. This going beyond is the higher third
of the Madhyamaka dialectic, the prajna-wisdom that's beyond language
and concepts.

For Wu-men (1183–1260), the great Chinese Master who compiled the

Wumenguan (*The Gateless Gate*, known in Japanese as *Mumonkan*), this going beyond means:

> One instant is eternity;
> eternity is the now.
> When you see through this one instant,
> you see through the one who sees.

Dunn and Jourdan have translated Sengcan's line as, "Go beyond both appearance and emptiness and find the unmoving center." This is a valuable practice perspective, for in Chan, at least, there is the tradition of cultivating the "unmoving center." It has its anatomical counterpart in the body, the lower abdomen (*hara* in Japanese; *tan-jien* in Chinese) where *chi* or energy is stored and cultivated. When this "center" is strong, it does not get moved by either the internal chatter or external phenomena. All of the aesthetic and martial arts in China, Japan, and Korea, such as calligraphy, archery, tai-chi, and so on, place extraordinary emphasis on this center in the body. In meditative traditions such as zazen, this center becomes both the causal agent and the repository of a radical transformation. It can even be argued that if this physical repository is not seen as an integral part of a radical transformation, any discussion of the latter is simply translational and self-deceptive.

The changes that appear to occur in the empty world we call real only because of our ignorance:

The phenomenal world and the psychological worlds are empty worlds because the units that make up these worlds have no own-being; they are all dependently arisen. If we take the changes that occur in these worlds to be "real" we end up making emotional and psychological investments, and thus feeling bereft when the return on the investment is not what we expect. Our ignorance is not seeing the dependently arisen nature of changes that are taking place all around us, and in us. None of this is "real" in the sense of having its own-being.

Any debate about "real" is really, as we have been discussing, about taking positions for "being" or "non-being," which, in turn, is an assertion or denial of one sort or another.

Do not search for the truth; only cease to cherish opinions:

Searching for the Truth-with-a-capital-*T* ends up only reinforcing the sense of a separate self. The realization or direct apprehension of the nature of things is transformative (within the mind-body *holos*). We have been conditioned to believe that there is a Truth out there, and each religion claims to have a revelation that has some sort of copyright on this Truth. For Chan and Buddhist traditions, by contrast, in the phenomena flowing endlessly like a mighty river there are only moments of realizations when the curtain of ignorance has been lifted and we are able to see clearly and directly that everything is dependently arisen, and nothing is self-sustaining. Radical transformation is indeed nothing more than ceasing to cherish opinions. We could, for example, have all kinds of opinions about the ever-changing flow of the river or we could simply watch the flow of the river to the point where the watcher, the watching, and the flow of the river merge into an undifferentiated experience. "Opinions" means taking a position for or against anything and everything. We may mistakenly believe a whole life is a sum total of these opinionated accumulations, not excluding our ideas, beliefs, and prejudices.

Not searching for the Truth and ceasing to cherish opinions are *not* catatonic states, but rather conscious, vigorous engagements with our opinionated accumulations. The Taoists would call it *wei wu-wei* or "the doing of not-doing," which is a proactive state of letting go of all views and opinions in a state of serenity or equanimity.

Dunn and Jourdan's translation of this line as, "Rather than focus on knowing the truth, simply cease to be seduced by your opinions" speaks forcefully to our habitual patterns and behavior. Each one of us gets so seduced by our opinions about things large and small that this seduction itself becomes one of the core organizing principles of our lives. Western culture especially puts so much emphasis on cultivating and expressing opinions that it becomes the only acceptable way to be in the world. What would it be like if we could train ourselves to softly note "this is the deluded mind at work" each time an opinion is formed in the mind?

Do not remain in the dualistic state; avoid such pursuits carefully:

The duality of self and the other is the basic split that causes us endless anguish. The use of the word "carefully" by Sengcan is important here in that it suggests a constant vigilance in the cultivation of mindfulness. An understanding of dualistic thinking and its long-term impact on the structure of consciousness is not a mere piece of information that we can tuck away someplace and retrieve for a coffeehouse discussion. The dualistic thinking must be avoided in each moment and every engagement; without careful attention it is all too easy to slide back without being aware of it.

When the separated self disappears, then, there is only the phenomena presenting itself to itself. This too must be remembered carefully in subsequent moments.

If there is even a trace of this and that, of right and wrong, the Mind-essence will be lost in confusion:

Equanimity is itself the Mind-essence. Earlier, we noted that Sengcan is using this "essence" of mind as the original stillness. In that sense, Mind-essence is illuminative rather than substantive. All categories of dualistic thinking have their own trajectories and stresses, and eventually cover up the original stress-less condition of mind. The original condition of the mind is equanimous, and this potentiality continues to exist regardless of how many layers of traces cover it up. To access this potentiality is to recover the original Mind-essence.

Although all dualities come from the One, do not be attached even to this One:

As we have seen earlier, there have been any number of Buddhist designations to describe what the Taoists mean by the "One": shunyata, Buddha-nature, Buddha-mind, No Mind, One Mind, Mind Essence, even Zero.

When we begin to explore the roots of multiplicity, we need to take great care that we are not simply trying to find a "Source" to which we can attach our separate self and have a sense of becoming "spiritual." The "Root," the "Source," the "One" are also Zero, shunyata. Any attachment to the One as self-validating, self-sustaining phenomenon does grave injury to the spirit of inquiry, to the possibility of radical transformation. In the bodhisattva model of the Mahayana, the aspiration to buddhahood requires emerging from the ghost cave of emptiness and functioning in the world with Avalokiteshvara's helping hands.

When the mind exists undisturbed in the Way, nothing in the world can offend:

By "offend" Sengcan here means the myriad habitual negative reactions that arise in response to aversion. Taking offense is a psychological function of the ego which is itself rooted in a dramatic sense of self-importance. But when one does not cling to anything, one also does not react negatively to anything. One sees the world of emptiness clearly and compassionately in its multiplicity and responds only in useful, skillful ways. When equanimity is firmly grounded in the Zero-ness of all things, the world of multiplicity loses its power to confuse or disturb.

This is not to say that one loses all capacity for seeing the suffering in the world. To the contrary, the bodhisattva dedicates his/her life to doing precisely the opposite. The hunger of a child, the various human-made holocausts, the social injustices, the biological pain of each existence, all evoke the compassion of the bodhisattva. Yet this evocation does not come from a place of "taking offense."

Rather, the bodhisattva sees all such situations of suffering as unwholesome, and employs whatever skillful means he or she can muster to address the situation. In other words, there is no personal anger in the bodhisattva's response to situations of suffering—only a skillful response balanced by wisdom and compassion.

And when a thing can no longer offend, it ceases to exist in the old way:

The Buddhist meditative traditions talk about training in the uprooting of defilements or unwholesome states of mind *(kilesas)*. This uprooting is a deconditioning of the conditioned mind; the process can be long or short, painful or relatively painless, depending on the person's karmic proclivities. It involves both a perceptual and relational shift; after all, our perception of a thing is integral to our relationship/reactivity to it. Earlier we talked about the empty boat coming toward a fisherman and his dramatically different perception and reaction to it after he realized it was empty: its actions ceased to offend him and in that moment his perception changed, and his letting go of his old reaction also caused the boat to cease existing in the old way. Ceasing to exist in the old way, then, is the end of reactivity put into place by an endless series of preferences, of likes and dislikes.

But the end of reactivity is not the goal in itself. The nature of human consciousness being what it is, it has to express itself in one way or another. When we train ourselves in not reacting, we are also training ourselves in a non-reactivity that is a proactive condition of being in the world. Non-reactivity, rather than being passive, is an active engagement with the world as much as reactivity is, although in a completely different direction. This is the *wei-wu-wei* of the Taoists.

When no discriminating thoughts arise, the old mind ceases to exist:

The old mind is the habitual, conditioned mind that operates through opinionated accumulations, through internal chatter. Its fuel is the addiction to discriminative tendencies to take and hold positions for and against each and all things. When this mind has been deconditioned to the extent that it does not engage in discriminative thought, it is a condition of nirvana, a cessation of the old conditioned mind. In nirvana, the sense of dukkha, which was a product of the conditioned mind in the first place, has been brought to a resolution. The mind of equanimity replaces the old mind of confusion and sorrow.

The question that has been asked of Zhuangzi by his biographer applies equally well to Sengcan and what he is trying to communicate:

> How exactly is the condition of spiritual lightness and freedom described by Zhuangzi [Chuang Tzu] to be reached? It is clear that, in his view, zealous striving and endeavour will achieve nothing. What seems to be required is much more like a letting go, the creation of a mental space or emptiness in which an awareness of the nature of the Dao can develop. Zhuangzi's True Man has to "unlearn" the ordinary ways of living and must cultivate a

consciousness that perceives the world afresh through a minute-to-minute questioning of every presupposition that has bound him or her in a false relationship with the world. Such a person is liberated from those unthinkingly acquired assumptions and is able to abandon the constructed social self, becoming free to inhabit nature as an element in it rather than as a separate entity pitted against it.[56]

When thought objects vanish, the thinking subject vanishes, as when the mind vanishes, objects vanish:

In radical transformation there's the transcendence of subject-object duality which in turn becomes the gateway for letting go of all clinging. An object of thought exists in a unique configuration as a result of the relationship the thinking subject brings to it. For another person, the same object of thought will have a different configuration because the other person's relationship to it will be different. The appearance of a mind-object in a certain configuration depends entirely on the thinking mind-subject. When the mind-subject is purified of its addictive habits of discrimination, the corresponding world of mind-objects disappears; when there is no world of mind-objects to support the habit, there is no thinking subject either. The consciousness is still there but it exists freely of dualistic or discriminatory notions.

Things are objects because of the subject (mind); the mind (subject) is such because of things (object):

Sengcan is here building on some very sophisticated theories of perception that have gone before him in the early Indian tradition, especially the Abhidharma, the compendium of Buddhist science of mind. Abhidharma was added as the third "basket" to the Pali Canon at the time of the third council (circa 250 B.C.E., during the reign of king Ashoka). The theories of perception and cognition in the Abhidharma continue to be of great interest to psychologists and philosophers even today. The school of Yogachara in medieval Indian Mahayana added its own theories of consciousness to the Abhidharma understanding and, as mentioned above, the Yogachara texts translated by Paramartha were very much a part of scholastic Buddhist discourse during Sengcan's lifetime. It is unlikely that Sengcan himself was familiar with these systematized theories of mind and perception, but it is not out of the question that meditation communities like Sengcan's may have been receiving a simplified version of these theories by word of mouth through itinerant monks. Of course, the Taoist tradition brought its own particular language to reflect on these issues of perception and subject-object dualities and people like Sengcan were beneficiaries of both systems of thought.

In experiencing the inner and outer worlds, we become "things" because of our minds peering out from within like a pair of eyes. In this peering out, we create "objects" by being objectively aware of them, and in the same way we make ourselves an object by positioning ourselves as a subject who is separate from the things it perceives including itself. The quality of self-consciousness gives us the illusion that this consciousness is separate from what it is observing or is conscious of. But when we look very closely, we find that this separation between subject and object is a language game.

As mentioned earlier, Chan tradition held a deep distrust of the role of language in creating this subject-object duality, and its basic premise was always that if language itself is transcended, the duality too will be transcended and one will reach a state of non-differentiation/oneness in which subject and object are not two. The subject is neither subject nor object; at the same time the object is not object either because its existence as "object" is determined by a misperception of the observer.

This is the old conundrum: "Does a tree make a noise when it falls into the forest while no one is around?" Any discussion about "noise" outside the personal experience of the hearer is an abstract and conceptual issue.

Similarly, in a deluded state, any and all conceptual categories of thought become the subject that then begins to reify the conditioned mind itself as the object of subjective thought, and the conditioned mind of course continues to see itself as the subject of objective thoughts. In short, this is a quick and easy path to sorrow and anguish.

The way out is to be constantly vigilant about how we use language dualistically in subject-object categories, and subsequently reify both. As Sengcan reminded us, this needs vigilance and careful and constant attention. When there is no subject aware of itself looking at an object as an object, and the object does not seek any validation through being observed by an observer, we find in our experience a here-now before all linguistic constructions.

Understand the relativity of these two and the basic reality: the unity of emptiness:

Any attempt at transcendence or liberation, at least in Buddhist traditions, must take into account that any object of thought is a figment of the perceiver's imagination, in the sense of being uniquely particularized by the perceiver. There is a distorted relationship between the two but both can and should find a resolution in the underlying shunyata in which subject is not object, nor is object subject; subject is neither subject nor object, and object is neither object nor subject. This "logic of emptiness" highlights the relationship of the two while at the same time negating any independent validation of either; both are emptied out in shunyata.

In practical terms, all of Buddha's teachings point to the nature of greed, hatred, and delusion, the constructs that undergird and rule our emotional and psychological lives. Training in mindfulness allows us to see that when, say, anger arises, it exists only as an object of thought in the subject-mind. When the subject-mind has the necessary conditions for anger to arise as a mind-state, it becomes reified and solidified as an object and assumes a life of its own. It becomes a causal agent for multiple varieties of further anger, greed, and delusion. But if the subject-mind is "empty" and does not contain the necessary conditions, the mind-state of anger will not arise in the first place, and even if it arises, it will be in a much milder form. A training in mindfulness will allow it to be exposed as a mind-state and prevent it from becoming a causal agent for further multiplying itself.

Here the logic of emptiness sees both the arising mind-state and the subject-mind as being in a dynamic relationship but both are essentially empty of any independent existence as causal agents. They function as seemingly causal agents only when mindfulness is not present, when one is confused as to the true nature of mind-states that keep arising one after the other.

*In this emptiness the two are indistinguishable, and each contains in itself the
whole world:*

Because the mind-states and subject-mind are in a fluid and dynamic
relationship with each other, it is impossible to draw a line that separates
subject-mind from its own contents which the subject mind, in delusion,
treats as independently existing objects. Once the subject and object have
found their resolution in shunyata and have been exposed as empty, neither
is privileged over the other. In fact, each loses all "traces" of itself and
becomes indistinguishable from the other.

Here experiments from quantum physics are worth considering: At any
given time light can manifest itself as wave or particle. However, before the
manifestation as wave or particle, each is indistinguishable in their unmanifest
aspect. This unmanifest aspect or source is pure energy, and pure energy itself
cannot be apprehended apart from the manifested wave or particle. Thus the
manifest is the unmanifest and contains within itself the entire universe of
the unmanifest. Since each manifest entity contains the entire unmanifest, it
is equal to and indistinguishable from all other manifests and must remain
unprivileged. If all multiplicity is unprivileged, even the One cannot be priv-
ileged because the One is undistinguishable from the multiplicity.

*If you do not discriminate between coarse and fine, you will not be tempted to
prejudice and opinion:*

None of Sengcan's discussion about subject and object is an abstract philo-
sophical argument. Its purpose is to bring us back to the basic issue of addic-
tion to preferences the way in which that addiction hinders equanimity.
When all tendencies to discriminate between this and that are brought to a
cessation, the habitual patterns of prejudice, opinion-making, and judgments
are also brought to an end. We must not minimize the difficulties of this let-
ting go; it's a never-ending process; easy to talk about, extremely difficult to
live by. But letting go of all longing and clinging naturally exposes the Mind-
essence of equanimity that has been there all along in the background.

We can read Sengcan's "coarse and fine" as referring to the mistaken con-
ceptual distinction between "Buddhas" and "ordinary people" or indeed
any antithetical conceptual distinction.

*To live in the Great Way is neither easy nor difficult, but those with limited views
are fearful and irresolute:*

My Zen teacher, when presented with complaints by his students about
difficulties of training and discipline, used to say, "You make things easy,
they are easy. If you make things difficult, they are difficult." He would fur-
ther say, "Don't make things easy, don't make things difficult. Just do it."
Easy and difficult are conceptual categories in our encounter with the phe-
nomenal world. We set up these categories in self-defining ways and habit-
uate ourselves to view the world through those definitions.

Equanimity as the Great Way is not a category or object of thought, but
rather an unfolding process. In our delusion, we might see it as a "task,"
something on our checklist, but in doing so we cause only grief for ourselves
as we continue to monitor our "progress" in the Great Way. We get caught
in the idea of time, and "progress in the Great Way" becomes an item of con-
sumption for the desirous habits of the subject-mind. Setting up the Great
Way as an object of thought will only result in fearfulness and irresolution
for there will always be bumps on the road when we cultivate the Great Way
but those bumps are just bumps. They are neither easy nor difficult.

*The faster they hurry, the slower they go, and clinging cannot be limited; and even
to be attached to the idea of enlightenment is to go astray:*

When we encounter difficulties in our lives, our natural tendency is to want
to get rid of them as quickly as we can—but the cultivation of equanimity
demands that we sit back, that we let the bumps in the road *be* bumps in the
road and not hold any opinion for or against them. It is easy to get into the
trap of thinking that if we hurry up we are going to get that much closer to
"enlightenment" that much sooner. But of course there can be no timetable
for "getting enlightened."

In the Zen tradition, this attempt to hurry up is called the "stink of Zen."
This stink invades the consciousness when one practices for the sake of
enlightenment in fundamentally self-referential ways so that one can call it
"my enlightenment." Next thing we know, "my enlightenment" is posi-
tioned against the enlightenment of the other person, and, of course, my
enlightenment is better or greater or deeper than the other person's. Self-

delusion does not get any denser than this. Any attachment to the idea of
enlightenment becomes a self-defeating, even destructive, proposition.

Just let things be in their own way, and there will be neither coming nor going:

Allowing things to manifest themselves according to their own nature is to
let the subject-self be at ease with the unfolding of phenomena. In this ease
there is no distorted perception that gets trapped in the appearance/coming
or disappearance/going of things; there is only the unfolding of things in
dependence on a complex network of causes and conditions. Lombardo
translates this line as, "Just let it be! In the end, nothing goes, nothing stays."
In the world of nature, as in samsara, the world of human conditioning,
there is constant transfiguration, rather than any concretized coming or
going of things. Each transfiguration has the residue of the previous, and
an insinuation of the next transfiguration.

*Obey the nature of things (your own nature), and you will walk freely and
undisturbed:*

In the human realm, because we don't understand our true nature, we
impose a "path" from outside and become prisoners of that path. Once we
understand that the nature of all things, including oneself, is dependent aris-
ing, we can have trust in teachings called shunyata or Buddha-nature or Tao
as a provisional template. The function of these teachings is nothing more,
or less, than showing us how to walk freely and undisturbed. A trust in
Buddha-nature means one is not trying to control the unfolding of things
according to one's own agenda but rather letting things unfold according to
their own dependently arisen nature. Obeying the nature of things means
letting go of any personal agenda. When one has let go of this agenda, there
is freedom and lack of disturbance because any disturbance is caused in the
first place by having an agenda that brings with it a sense of control. With-
out any agenda or sense of control, every day is a good day. There's no "bad"
day because one has no investment in how things will unfold.

    Zen tradition talks often of the mirror as a metaphor for true nature. The
mirror reflects whatever appears in front of it, fully and without holding

anything back. When there is nothing in front of it, it just simply is what it has always been, an empty mirror. In our human experience, helping someone in front of us is an expression of our true nature. if someone is hungry, we give them food; if someone is thirsty, we give them water. Hunger and thirst are not, and need not be, matters of abstract debate. Our spontaneous and helpful response is a condition of "walking freely and undisturbed" precisely because we function in the world through helpful responses rather than abstract concepts.

The Great Way is a metaphor just as "walking freely and undisturbed [on the Great Way]" is a metaphor for a mind that remains balanced and does not get pulled one way or another in any and every situation. This is the great equanimity of the Buddhadharma and the Tao.

When thought is in bondage the truth is hidden, for everything is murky and unclear, and the burdensome practice of judging brings annoyance and weariness:

A thought is in bondage when it is a conceptualized abstraction. Abstract concepts don't reveal the truth of things. On the other hand, they have the habit of proliferating to the extent that everything becomes murky and confused. This, unfortunately, is our human condition where we try to sort out the truth of things through verbal constructions within verbal constructions. Over a period of time, this habit becomes wearisome and confusing. We feel stressed because abstract conceptualization does not seem to bring any solace beyond a momentary sense of self-importance. Our opinions come into conflict with the opinions of others and we judge our opinions as better (or occasionally less good) than others' opinions. This is the basic condition of ignorance or delusion *(avidya)* that the Buddha proposed as the ground of all dependent-arising in the second noble truth. We all have the delusion, to varying degrees, that our thoughts represent some sort of reality. What we don't usually understand is that all thoughts are constructions and are not necessarily useful tools in understanding reality. We get a direct glimpse into the nature of things when we let go of all abstract conceptualizations and allow the internal chatter to deconstruct. When this happens and our abstract thought becomes replaced with thoughts grounded in the reality of shunyata-wisdom, our thought is no longer in bondage.

The working of the internal chatter puts enormous acquisitive pressures on our lives, and we fail to see the truth of dependent arising in things that we are trying to acquire and hold on to. Our investment in things, our agenda in controlling the unfolding of things makes for very murky and unclear perceptions of ourselves and things of the world. The constant pressure of having things work according to our plans forces a way of being in the world where we are judging the outcome of each unfolding, and getting annoyed if things don't unfold the way we want them to. It's a cause of general weariness and confusion.

What benefit can be derived from distinctions and separations?:

Living in a mode that makes distinctions and separations between this and that according to one's own predilections, the average person sees the pursuit of food, sex, sleep, wealth, objects, or fame as benefits that will make life worthwhile and fulfilling. Little does the average person realize the annoyance and weariness that comes from a headlong pursuit of these presumed rewards, or even the ultimate pointlessness of these pursuits.

We all have the arrogance that we are smart enough to escape the negative results of these pursuits, and that we can do what other people are not able to do: have our cake and eat it too. The experience of each person in each generation has been that real life just doesn't work that way. Equanimity is not to be found in these pursuits, in the world of internal chatter, in judgments and discriminations, in wanting things to be this way and not that way.

If you wish to move in the One Way, do not dislike even the world of sense and ideas:

Equanimity is not a rejection of anything. It is knowing that putting your hand in the fire is not a profitable enterprise; knowing that a headlong pursuit of food, sex, sleep, fame, and fortune will only result in dismay and weariness. Equanimity allies itself with a quality of restraint in one's life that is not based on dislike or rejection of anything but is grounded rather in the wisdom-experience of self-knowing and a knowing of the world.

There may perhaps even be an echo in Sengcan of the basic Chinese dis-agreements with the Indian ascetic traditions. These ascetic traditions emerged in ancient India as alternative spirituality to Brahmanic claims to cosmic knowledge. But, over centuries, as Brahmanic religiosity became more and more rigid and puritanical, the ascetic traditions also grew corre-spondingly rigid and puritanical through symbiosis. The rejection of the world of senses in this puritanical framework was never well-received by the Chinese who were, first and foremost, pragmatic and earthy people. The Chinese could accept the ascetic practices as a means of acquiring super-natural powers but the worldview that saw the world of senses as "impure" did not move the Chinese very much. For the Taoists, "pure" and "impure" were yet another trap of conceptualized thinking.

Chan is a movement away from the world-rejection of Indian Buddhism and this is echoed clearly in Taoist naturalism. This affinity with the world of nature is a counterpoint to notions of purity and impurity whenever they crept into their inherited Indian Buddhism. It accounts for a creative tension within Chan. A Zen poem declares unequivocally:

> Good and evil have no self-nature;
> Holy and unholy are empty names;
> Spring comes, grass grows by itself.
> In front of the [sense] door is the land of stillness and light.[57]

Indeed, to accept them fully is identical with true Enlightenment:

This is perhaps one of the most crucial lines in the poem. Acceptance here is not used in opposition to rejection but rather in the sense of letting things unfold according to their self-nature, their thing-ness. This kind of acceptance is the middle way between indulgence and rejection. Accepting the world of senses and ideas refers to the radically transformed perspective in which one sees the dependent arising of things, sees their impermanence, sees their lack of self-abiding, and has compassion for those who make investment in this fleeting world. Thus one has no compulsion to indulge in or reject this world. The world becomes transparent in this radical transformation.

Dunn and Jourdan have translated the two lines above as, "Use your senses to experience reality, for they are part of your empty mind. This

empty mind takes note of all it perceives and is guided by its sensing needs."
This points to the crucial understanding that the senses themselves can be
a skillful tool to discern the nature of reality. After all, we are human animals
and, compared to other animals, we have the freedom to choose between
either being prisoners of our skeletal and brain systems or using these very
systems to understand ourselves skillfully.

The wise person strives to no goals but the foolish person fetters himself:

In the perspective of radical transformation there can be no compulsion to
have any goals in the conventional sense. The world of the average person
is premised on the pursuit of rewards because one sees these as goals that
will bring benefits that make life "meaningful." Of course, each person's
definition of meaning is elastic and self-serving, but radical transformation
makes the world transparent so that one sees that there is no inherent mean-
ing in things and that all goal-setting in the hope of some benefit is a fruit-
less pursuit.

The "foolish person" is the consumer par excellence who derives his/her
identity from consumptive accumulations. He/she does not see that these
very consumptive accumulations become fetters and keep one in bondage.
All consumption is based on some conscious or unconscious goal-seeking.
The "wise person" restrains himself/herself from such pursuits. The foolish
or the ignorant are bound to emotional choices that in turn attach them
more fiercely to their ignorance. The wise person, on the other hand, walks
through life unswayed and nonreactive, yet free to act compassionately and
with equanimity.

*There is one Dharma, not many; distinctions arise from the clinging needs of the
ignorant:*

Dharma is defined in many different ways within the Buddhist tradition. It
is the teaching of the historical Buddha; it is also the cosmic law underlying
all phenomena in the universe. The two aspects are connected by the under-
standing that this "law" existed already before the birth of the historical
Buddha, who reformulated this universal truth in his own language. It is in

the Dharma in this sense that a Buddhist takes refuge. This law or dharma, as reformulated by the historical Buddha, is the dependent-arising of things. As we have discussed earlier, Nagarjuna equated dependent-arising with shunyata. A necessary corollary of dependent-arising is transience *(anitya)* and nonsubstantiality *(anatman)*, both of which are folded back into Nagarjuna's shunyata teaching. For Sengcan, shunyata is the wider framework within which he speaks of Dharma. It is the realm of nondifferentiation, of a holographic whole, as we have been discussing. When one is ignorant of this underlying dharma, one clings to things according to one's preferences. When one has a taste of this dharma, one lets go of all clinging. In letting go of all clinging, one also lets go of all preferences. One remains in an equanimous state regardless of how the phenomena are presenting it to the senses.

In equanimity, all distinctions find their resolution; the process of longing-clinging-becoming comes to an end. The "taste" of this resolution is nirvana: the cessation of all longing and clinging; this taste is the "peace that passeth understanding." Behind the world of distinctions, there is only dependent-arising, shunyata, Dharma, the Tao, the world of freedom. Freedom is not anything abstract but a being-in-becoming free from longing and clinging.

To seek Mind with the (discriminating) mind is the greatest of all mistakes:

One of the critical insights of the Buddhist wisdom traditions has been that you cannot think your way out of your thinking. The trap created by language is an endless feedback loop. To break out of the trap requires a quantum jump rather than a linguistic structure. The genius of Chan was to discover that language could be used to turn itself back upon itself; in that sense, Chan tradition has a distrust of language but not a rejection. It is convinced that language can be used in creative ways to see its own limitations. The most vivid examples of this creativity are the anecdotal encounters preserved in koans between various Chan personages.

A monk came to the famous master Zhaozhou, and asked, "What is Buddha [Mind]?" Zhaozhou's reply was, "Three pounds of flax!" Zhaozhou was reminding the questioner that he was trying to seek the "Mind" with his conditioned mind in the assumption that a knowing of the [Buddha/One]

Mind is in the realm of verbal understanding. Zhaozhou used a kind of verbal judo to turn the whole verbal exchange on its head. The Mind (Buddhamind, True Self, the Tao, and so on) becomes transparent only in a radical transformation that has nothing to do with verbal or linguistic understanding. The prajna-wisdom is a transcendence of all verbal knowing, for such a knowing is limited to knowing the properties of things and not very helpful when it comes to the Tao or shunyata.

Rest and unrest derive from illusion; with enlightenment there is no liking or disliking:

We have a tendency to blame our condition of unrest/stress on external conditions: "If only this or that were different I would be perfectly content." In our opposite-thinking, we create a condition of "rest" as the absence of "unrest" but what we are really saying is that we want the stress to go away. We don't want the notion of "rest" to go away because that's our fallback position. We are equally unwilling to see that unrest derives from the imperatives of longing-clinging-becoming in our lives. We somehow have the illusion that if undesirable stresses will go away, we can continue to hold on to those things that we desire. But, as we have been discussing, if equanimity becomes calcified as an identifiable place of "resting," it becomes both a cause and result of one's ignorance. Authentic equanimity means a complete letting go of all likes and dislikes, without any traces remaining. Only then does equanimity become a place of resting. So long as "rest" and "unrest" are categories of conceptual self-referentiality, one moves farther and farther away from equanimity.

All dualities come from ignorant inference; they are like dreams or flowers in the air: foolish to try to grasp them:

All our preferences are based on some kind of assignation of "value" to each preference. We impute a certain value to things of the world and make an investment accordingly. These assignations are nothing but projections of our deep conditioning; this is our delusion, our ignorance. We delude ourselves into thinking that our preferences are rational, independent, and worthwhile, all the while ignorant of the underlying processes of inferences and projections.

The classic example of inference is from the Indian philosophical tradition: a person sees a snake-like shape in the dark, and gets frightened out of his wits. When he lights a lamp and looks closely he finds that what he thought to be a snake was actually a coiled up rope. But the fright had a truly affective impact on the mind-body system; the inference of the rope as snake brought up the primordial fear of death and dying.

In the same way, when we live in the world of dualities and make investments in those dualities based on preferences for likes and dislikes, we are letting each preference, and its inherent inference as something of value, impact our mind-body system in injurious ways. When the illuminative nature of prajna-wisdom is brought to bear upon these preferences, inferences, and projections, they are found to be dependently arisen and are seen nothing more than dreams or flowers in the air already in the process of falling down.

Gain and loss, right and wrong: such thoughts must finally be abolished at once:

Once we see that all ideas about gain and loss, right and wrong are nothing more than dream-projections, it is possible to drop them as a frame of reference. We train ourselves, instead, to use language more carefully and creatively so that these dualities are seen as nothing more than conceptual constructs without any inherent meaning to them. Chan and Buddhist traditions have never been comfortable with the equivalent of biblical notions of "right" and "wrong" or "just" and "unjust." Such thoughts are seen as impediments to clear seeing, to making the world transparent through radical transformation. Just as dreams confuse our reality of the waking state, so do the dualities of right and wrong, gain and loss disturb the inner calm. All of these dualistic distinctions are like throwing rocks into a still pond and disturbing its surface of calmness.

If the eye never sleeps, all dreams will naturally cease. If the mind makes no discriminations, the ten thousand things are as they are, of single essence:

The sleeping eye here can be seen as a metaphor for living in ignorance, and dreams as a metaphor for samsara. In the Buddha's teaching, ignorance has a central place in the explication of how the wheel of samsara is constructed. The Buddha called it the truth of dependent-arising and it points to samsara as the construct-effect of causal factors that are ultimately rooted in ignorance. This ignorance is not understanding the true nature of things of the world; that lack of understanding puts into place the compulsive cycle of longing-clinging-becoming. More than one Zen teacher has pointed out that without training in mindfulness, one sleepwalks through life.

A "buddha" is a person who wakes up. In sleepwalking through life, one is subject to rebirth in samsara and suffering. The hold of longing-clinging-becoming continues to be inexorably powerful life after life after life. By contrast, the eye that never sleeps can be seen as a metaphor for living in transparency. Just as the eye that never sleeps will not dream, so too living in wakefulness will put a stop to sleepwalking through life. Being awake, one is free of the bondage of samsara, no longer subject to rebirth in it. This is the Buddha's template for nirvana.

This ceasing of ignorance is not a forced effort; it is not a goal to be realized as an enterprise of resume-building. It happens naturally in a state of transparency without any kind of forcing. This transparency is the One Mind in which nothing is forced. It is an a priori condition of mind that can be experienced existentially but does not lend itself very well to verbal or conceptual reification.

To understand the mystery of this One-essence is to be released from all entanglements:

To see everything the way this poet is seeing is to free oneself from all entanglements, which are the headlong pursuit of food, sex, sleep, wealth, and fame. They bind us to the world of projections, inferences, preferences, discriminations, and self-gratification. They constitute the realm of samsara, dukkha, unsatisfactoriness. When one has penetrating insight into the dependently arising nature of all entanglements, one has the cognitive, affective, and behavioral thrust for "opening the hand of thought," as Kocho Uichiyama puts it.

Opening the hand of thought is the metaphorical opposite of holding the hand in a tight fist at all times, grabbing, one hopes, the "desirable" entanglements. But a clenched fist becomes painful and constrictive after a while. Similarly, trying to hold on to desirable entanglements proves to be equally painful and constrictive. Opening the hand of thought means that even in the midst of pressures generated by longing-clinging-becoming, one is disciplined enough not to close one's hand around these entanglements and lock it into a fist. An "open hand" is not a forced, discriminatory rejection of things of the world but rather "seeing through" them as constructions without any self-abiding structural core to them. Shunyata perspective is the liberation of the conditioned mind.

Uchiyama also writes, "[Opening the hand of thought means] study and practice [of] the Buddha-dharma only for the sake of Buddha-dharma, not for the sake of human emotions or worldly ideas."[58] Sengcan's poem is in the service of liberation, and not for the sake of finding consolation in entanglements.

When all things are seen equally the timeless Self-essence is reached:

From the perspective of shunyata, all things share equally the same nature, of dependent-arising. This self-essence is "no-essence" or the "original essence" in the sense that it has no properties into which it can be broken down. Without any properties, it is not quantifiable in temporal or spatial terms; it becomes "timeless" and "spaceless." When the subject-self sees the dependently-arising nature of all things, including the subject-self and the object-self, one gains awareness into the realm of the timeless and the spaceless.

Lombardo translates this line as, "See the ten thousand things as equal and return to your original nature." This translation speaks more clearly to the training in mindfulness. If no distinction is made either between one thought and the other, or one external phenomenon and the other, one is able to remain in the original equanimous quality of mind that's always present below the surface.

No comparison or analogies are possible in this causeless, relationless state:

Comparisons are possible only when we make distinction between one thing and the other. When no distinctions are made and no values assigned, comparisons are not possible. In a more refined understanding, all things are arising and passing away in dependence on other things. The timelessness and spacelessness of this dependent-arising defies comparisons or analogies; whatever we can think of by way of comparison is within our own human experience of time and space. It does not mean that it cannot be experienced; it's only that any comparisons or analogies are the domain of verbal expressions, and language is inadequate to express the experience of something that is free of the workings of time and space.

Conversely, when we use comparison or analogies we fragment our experience into parts but our experience of equanimity or One Mind trancends all conceptual and even causal relations. The network of causes and conditions that has led to the realization of equanimity is on one level a causal factor, but the discernible quality of *causelessness* in the personal experience of equanimity makes any discussion of "cause" rather meaningless precisely because that quality of experience cannot be broken down into parts or relations.

Consider movement stationary and the stationary in motion, both movement and rest disappear:

We have been exploring the noxious hold that opposite-thinking has in our lives. In our dualistic thinking, we create categories and posit them in opposition to each other; we delude ourselves into thinking that each category has some independent quality unique to itself and not available to its opposite category. The classical Taoist symbol of *yin* and *yang* shows the limitation and paucity of this dualistic approach. In this symbol, yin and yang each has distinct qualities (light and dark) but each carries a "trace" of the other; at no point therefore is yin wholly yin or yang wholly yang. It is at all times yin-yang, regardless of the dominant focus on yin or yang in any given moment. In yin-yang, both yin and yang "disappear" as indivisible yin or indivisible yang. There is a sense here in which all opposites are transcended by the unity of the whole that exists without opposites.

The disappearance of the opposites is not a condition of annihilation but the "higher third" of Madhyamaka that each thing carries a trace of the other. To insist that each thing exists autonomously without a trace of the other is a misguided perspective. "I" always includes the "not-I" because it is through its self-awareness of "not-I" that I defines itself as "I."

When such dualities cease to exist Oneness itself cannot exist:

When dualistic thinking is deconstructed, the truth of dependent arising is seen as pervading all phenomena. All dualistic categories are linguistic constructions, and do not accurately represent the phenomenon as carrying a trace of the other. If even Oneness is considered within the framework of language, it will stand in opposition to "multiplicity" and both will become linguistic constructions. If Oneness is understood here as shunyata or dependent-arising, it follows that all multiplicities carry a trace of dependent-arising, but dependent-arising as Oneness cannot exist outside of the traces found within the multiplicities.

To this ultimate finality no law or description applies:

The ultimate finality here is not related to the First Cause controversy of the Western philosophical tradition but rather to the condition wherein dualities cease to exist. What is it like? Chan teachers realized early on that to try to describe the nondual condition in positive language is a self-defeating enterprise, and they wisely focused on a methodology of "questioning" rather than providing answers or descriptions. In other words, there are no descriptive allusions to that ultimate nondual state other than metaphors. The "taste" of this condition is for the subject-self to discover within its own experience.

The Buddha did come up with the designation of *pratitya-samyutpada*, the "law" of dependent-arising, to describe this ultimate finality but this designation is not a law in the conventional or ideological sense. It is a way of explaining why things are the way they are, and it can be, and must be, verified in one's own experience. We find that all multiplicities are dependently arisen, and we also find that dependent-arising, being a no-thing, is not in the domain of multiplicities, and therefore eludes any notion of thing-in-itself. The law of dependent-arising is not an ontology just as the law of gravity in physics is not an ontology.

The Buddha chose to describe the ultimate finality as dependent-arising, whereas Laozi said of it, "The Tao is that which cannot be described; that which can be described is not the Tao." Nagarjuna described this ultimate finality as shunyata, as a synonym for dependent-arising, and Chan teachers used the Tao as a synonym for shunyata. None is making an absolutist claim for an ultimate finality, however.

An alternate translation of this line from Lombardo reads, "In true nature there are no goals or plans." He also translates the following line as, "In the mind before thinking, no effort is made." Together, these two lines point more to training in mindfulness and its context. A goal-less, plan-less way of being in the world becomes the canvas upon which lack of self-centered striving paints a master drawing. In Taoist terms, the Tao becomes the wu-wei, and vice versa.

For the unified mind in accord with the Way all self-centered striving ceases:

To actually live our lives equanimously in accordance with the shunyata perspective requires a seamless integration of the cognitive, affective, and behavioral factors. Thus the "three higher trainings" in the Buddha's eightfold path address each of these different aspects: *prajna or wisdom* addresses cognitve transformation, *samadhi or training in mindfulness* addresses affective transformation, and *shila or wholesome conduct* brings about behavioral transformation through the observance of the ethical precepts of right action, right speech, and right livelihood. The prajna-wisdom of shunyata informs the disciplined training in meditation as to its goals and aspirations; the deep experience of meditation becomes shunyata as a felt-experience and this felt-experience informs one's behavior in the world. If the felt-experience is truly of seeing through the limitation of longing-clinging-becoming, it has the effect of making one transparent. No longer does one operate under the delusion of a separate self. But this felt-experience is not abiding in time and space, and requires constant mindfulness to keep itself vital and relevant.

In the transparency of nonself, there is no forced striving since the affective structure and the wisdom of nonself is already in accord with the Way, having transcended all dualities. It has become One Mind which is also No-Mind which is also Great Mind. In this One Mind all striving fueled by a separate self has come to a stop. In the One mind there is no compulsion to leave a "trace" and one becomes naturally "traceless"—while the One Mind itself becomes the true dwelling place. Ikkyu, the famous Japanese Zen master from the fourteenth century, puts it beautifully and simply:

> Cover your path
> with fallen pine needles
> so no one will be able
> to locate your true dwelling place.

Doubts and irresolutions vanish, and life in true faith is possible:

In an authentic transformation, by becoming transparent, one has a sense of ease of being in the world, of moving without doubts or irresolutions about the self since the self has been seen through as nonself. The doubts and irresolutions were, in the first place, a product of a sense that there needs to be some "reality" behind "I"/"me"/"mine." This is the sense in which the Buddha used avidya or confusion as the first link in the chain of dependent-arising. The transcendence of avidya is clear-seeing or transparency which means that these categories have become transparent and are seen as constructs of our conditioning without a core or abiding "own-being" behind them. Thus seen, they cease creating the sense of sorrow or anguish through which we habitually live our lives. But this seeing is possible only in a genuine transparency and it is in this transparency that one puts one's "faith." There is a trust in one's own experience and in the shunyata-wisdom that arises within one's own experience. True faith in the Buddhadharma is, for Sengcan, possible only when one validates the teachings for oneself.

With a single stroke we are freed from bondage; nothing clings to us and we hold to nothing:

The bondage has always been of longing-clinging-becoming. When the feedback loop of transformation, and trust in it, works effectively, we can move in the world with an open hand rather than with a clenched fist. We can move even in a crowded marketplace without grabbing on to anything. If we don't grab on to anything, nothing clings to us, and this facilitates keeping open the hand of thought.

The second half of this line "nothing clings to us and we hold to nothing" has been translated by most other translators in the sense of forgetting and remembering.

Suzuki: "Nothing is retained now, nothing is to be memorized."

Sheng-yen: "Nothing lingers behind, nothing can be remembered."

Waley: "Nothing is left over, nothing remembered."

Blyth: "Nothing remains behind; there is not anything we must remember."

Lu: "When all this is thrown away, there's nothing to remember."

The sense of this phrase is that when we truly let go of all clinging, the remembrance of things past do not continue to haunt us. After all, it is through our memory that we hold on to things and things can cling to us only when we hold on to them. Things don't have their own-being but they continue to "exist" only in our memory as part of the inventory of various clingings. A clinging finds its fuel in longing and when there's no longing, there is no place for it to cling.

All is empty, clear, self-illuminating, with no exertion of the mind's power:

This is the world of "transparency," to which access is granted through the prajna-wisdom of shunyata, supported by the deep samadhi experience of nonseparation. This world is self-illuminated because it has shed all layers of bondage of longing-clinging-becoming, and has allowed the deepest sense of ease to emerge. This sense of ease is not the result of any exertion on the part of conditioned mind but rather of letting go. When there is neither "self" nor "other," awareness simply is. In this simply being itself, awareness is empty yet luminous. No effort is made and none is needed for this awareness to be anything other than what it is. The Buddha spoke of this awareness as,

> This mind, O monks, is luminous, and is freed from adventitious defilements. The instructed noble disciple understands this as it really is; therefore for him there is mental development.[59]

This luminosity expresses itself only in the transparent space of shunyata-emptiness. This transparent space is expressed wonderfully by Shinkichi Takahashi, a twentieth-century Zen poet from Japan:

> The wind blows hard among the pines,
> toward the beginning
> of an endless past.
> Listen: you've heard everything.[60]

Here thought, feeling, knowledge, and imagination are of no value:

The space of this luminosity is not nihilistic and yet it does not depend on the contents of the conditioned mind: the universe of thoughts, feelings, knowledge, and imagination that we carry with us at all times in such desperate ways. The challenge here is not to turn the experience of this luminosity into yet another category of thought, feeling, knowledge, and imagination. The difficulty of this challenge cannot be undermined. Almost all mystics in all religious traditions have failed as communicators of the nondual experience in significant ways because they have invariably tried to describe it within the framework of their old conditioning. In the process they have turned this indescribable luminosity into yet another category.

In the world of transparency, there is a seeing-through of all conditioned, self-centered thoughts, feelings, and imagination. Within the Chan framework of practice, one learns to be present to this moment of primordial experience without appropriating it into a schema of linguistic construction. The space between the primordial experience and its appropriation is the time-space of liberation.

In this world of suchness there is neither self nor other-than-self:

In this space of luminosity there is no self-consciousness of self as subject-self, object-self, nonself, not-nonself, or other-than-self. Perhaps an appropriate metaphor here is the consciousness of the baby when it is inside the mother's womb. We know from advances in medical sciences that the baby has consciousness but no self-consciousness in the sense of being conscious of its separateness from the environment in which it floats. This is one aspect of the world of suchness. In it, no one thing is privileged over the other; in it, all things are accepted equally. This is not to imply, however, that suchness exists as a metaphysical entity beyond the non-discriminating consciousness.

Lombardo translates "suchness" as the "true Dharma world" in this sentence. An alternate understanding of the true Dharma world would be that of Dharmakaya. In Indian Mahayana Buddhism, Dharmakaya is indeed synonymous with both *suchness* and *shunyata*.

To come directly into harmony with this reality, just simply say when doubt arises, "Not two":

To allow things to exist equally in their suchness is to be in tune with the harmony of things in their thing-ness. To be in harmony with the thing-ness of things is the non-privileging of one over the other, and that non-privileging is expressed as "not two." Things don't need to be qualified by their opposite. In its thing-ness each thing is both itself and its opposite and finds a resolution in the nondual shunyata. Sengcan is reminding us to remember the nondual shunyata nature of things by the signifier "not-two" whenever we are confused about the nature of reality. In this sense, "not-two" becomes a mantra that one can use to re-stabilize oneself when beset with doubt and confusion. However, this mantra is not to be used as a rote but as a clarifier of the empty nature of things.

At times we may imagine that "practice" is something esoteric, something imparted in secret and kept secret. Buddhist and Chan methodologies of practice are rooted in a simple remembering to return to breath awareness. This remembering is itself the "practice" and it can be remembered at any time, any place. The Zen phrase of "returning to the source" has the simple, exquisite existential template of remembering to be aware of the breath. Whatever fruits come out of this awareness (such as tranquillity or equanimity) are just fruits and we don't need to reify these fruits in any way. Remembering to return to the present moment is the key in the liberation of the mind. It sounds simple but it's an extraordinarily difficult thing to do. We forget so easily whenever we get caught up in the proliferation of our own internal chatter. Just remembering to say "not two" is a way to cut through all the doubts and confusions. It can be a practice tool to remind ourselves that the observing self is not separate from the observed phenomena.

In this "not two" nothing is separate, nothing is excluded:

The awareness that is able to locate itself in the "not two" modality assumes an essentially holographic perspective in which each thing contains everything and is contained in everything else; nothing is separate and nothing is excluded. To adopt the "not-two" perspective is to see all multiplicities falling back into an undifferentiated *holos* or shunyata in which all boundaries and definitions of each manifestation are lost and absorbed into the undifferentiated whole that is the One Mind in Sengcan's poem.

No matter when or where, enlightenment means entering this truth:

To be radically transformed is to see all things in the entire cosmos as existing in original harmony. When the conditioned mind is transcended, it becomes One Mind, the Tao, and it becomes the Source in which all things are contained. The condition of One Mind is its nonfragmentation because it does not make distinctions. This truth of nonfragmentation is not anything esoteric but rather a condition of not making distinctions.

With this line, Sengcan seems to ratchet up the intensity a bit. Enlightenment for him means entering the truth of nonduality. Nonduality cannot be an intellectual or linguistic construct for that would be inauthentic. There has to be an underlying experience in which all duality has come to a cessation. In Mahayana Buddhist understanding, this is the truth of the experience of nirvana: a cessation of duality. But this truth cannot be objectified or codified.

Moreover, by using the words, "No matter when or where," Sengcan is pointing to the ever-present potentiality for awakening. The later Chan tradition kept itself open to this potentiality in every mundane activity of daily life.

The premise of Chan is that each person is capable of entering the potentiality of not-two at any time, in any place. Lombardo's translation of this line as, "Enlightened beings everywhere all enter this source" brings in a slightly different perspective to what we have been discussing.

And this truth is beyond extension or diminution in time or space:

It is the experience of most people in an intensive meditation retreat (or, if they are fortunate, in the mundane events of daily life) that there are moments when one touches a place before time and space. These are moments of truth-realizations but they are not appropriated as truth-statements. Rather there is a prelinguistic intuitive realization before the constructs of time and space intrude. This realization does not get expanded or diminished by the working of time and space, is independent of how the conditioned mind may misconstrue it later on.

It also means that the "source" or "truth" is beyond time and space. The source here is the original empty nature, which is luminous and quiescent but ever-present below the surface. This source does not get diminished or enhanced in time or space. The "law" of dependent-arising, and the empty nature of phenomena, remain true whether or not things are manifesting themselves in time and space.

In it a single thought is ten thousand years:

When time is no longer able to exert its usual control in the unconditioned or One Mind, the distinction between one moment and ten thousand years is lost. Within the conditioned mind, time has become a "thing," a measurement that validates itself in relationship to other adjacent measurements. But the *experience* of time is different for each person, a subjective phenomenon. For a musician, deeply immersed in the creation of music, time stands "still" but passes very quickly; for an office worker wanting to leave the

office on the dot, time also stands still but passes very slowly. As T. S. Eliot
wrote,

> Time present and time past
> Are both perhaps present in time future,
> And time future contained in time past.
> If all time is eternally present
> All time is unredeemable.
> What might have been is an abstraction
> Remaining a perpetual possibility
> Only in a world of speculation.
> What might have been and what has been
> Point to one end, which is always present.[61]

If all time is now, ten thousand years are contained in this now; and this
now is contained in each moment of the next ten thousand years. If we are
truly grounded in the eternal-now, there is no bondage in us from the past
or the future. In our human experience, we are always a prisoner of remem-
brance of things past and speculation of things future. Past and future have
their uses in academia as tools of learning but our humanity does not need
to be constantly oppressed by these linear concepts.

*Emptiness here, emptiness there, but the infinite universe stands always before
your eyes:*

In the same way that ten thousand years are contained in the now-moment,
the entire universe is also contained in each dust particle. The shunyata-
emptiness of dependent-arising is here as well as everywhere and every-
when. In the inherent emptiness of each now-moment, the entire universe
stands deconstructed before our eyes in all the now-moments, even if we
cannot see through its veils with our conditioned minds. In the now-time
there is the entire space-time; and space-time, freed of the working of time
alone, is the entire universe, indivisible and whole. It is spread out always
and everywhere.

When we touch a place that's before time and space it's a moment of com-
plete emptying out, and even though everything has been emptied out, the

infinite universe stands there before us, not as something annihilated but as something pristine that has been stripped of layers of dust and grime. This is the universe-as-Dharmakaya formulation of Mahayana Buddhism. A clear and direct seeing of this universe-as-Dharmakaya is possible only by an individual consciousness that has been equally stripped of all layers of internal chatter. When this purified consciousness-as-Dharmakaya sees the universe-as-Dharmakaya, it really is a case of Dharmakaya seeing itself in a mirror.

Infinitely large and infinitely small: no difference, for definitions have vanished and no boundaries are seen:

The definitions and measurements that normally obtain in the manifested world of phenomena lose their distinctions and boundaries in the openness of shunayta. In the shunyata-holograph in which every minute division reflects the infinite whole, things cannot be judged by conventional definitions and measurements.

So too with being and non-being:

In our earlier discussion of *bhava* as "being-in-becoming," we noted that phenomena are processes rather than concrete entities; as processes, they cannot be judged by conventional boundaries and definitions. Lombardo and Suzuki translate this line as, "What is, is the same as what is not; what is not is the same as what is"; Lu translates it as, "Is and is not are the same; For what is not, equals is"; Things are same or not-same only when perceived as concrete entities; as processes they lose all definitions of sameness or not-sameness. They are simultaneously both same and not-same. The definitional imperatives are only a function of the conditioned mind and the world of multiplicities. In the One Mind, where the conditioned mind with its multiplicities is transcended, things are "thing-ness," first and foremost, beyond definitions of this or that.

Don't waste time in doubts and arguments that have nothing to do with this:

If one sees directly into the nature of things, there is no point in arguing about definitions and boundaries that have nothing to do what is directly seen or experienced. Again, this is the experience of the mystic, and arguments are a function of one conditioned mind trying to convince another conditioned mind.

The experience of One Mind has nothing to do with these arguments; doubts and arguments obtain in the realm of provisional statements. This is the avidya (confusion, ignorance) the Buddha pointed to. The experience of One Mind is the experience of equanimity itself; it is not an ontology that needs to be proved.

One thing, all things: move among and intermingle, without distinction:

Lombardo and Suzuki translate this line succinctly as, "One is all, All is one," which reinforces the holographic perspective we have been using. And yet we need to be careful that we don't label this nonduality of "One is All, All is One" according to our conditioning. This is where most of the mystics go awry because they fall back upon the familiar language and assume that this experience of the nondual must fit into the language of their religious culture. For Sengcan it's enough to ground oneself in choiceless awareness in a spaciousness that is beyond time and space and where things move and intermingle among each other without distinctions. Once it is realized that what is and what is not are equals (both being conceptual) there is no need to be sorrowful about anything.

To live in this realization is to be without anxiety about non-perfection:

This realization is the liberated perspective that is an antidote to *dukkha* or the sense of anxiety, of incompleteness, of non-perfection. In the Chan tradition, One Mind is synonymous with True Self, and in the realization of True Self there is a transcendence of the fragmented, conditioned self. Because True Self is synonymous with awakening to the truth of this moment, it cannot identify with any of the features of the conditioned self whose modality is of anguish, *dukkha*.

Perfection and nonperfection are conceptual categories. To realize the unreality of the conceptual is to break open the mold of the value system that speaks of the perfect and the not-perfect. In the holographic mode, where each tiny piece is the whole, the question of perfection or nonperfection becomes meaningless. In their suchness, each thing is complete as it is; in its suchness, the entire universe is complete as it is. This is something we can trust wholeheartedly. But this trust cannot be forced; it has to come out of pure experience.

One of the earlier lines in the poem taught "The Great Way is perfect like space where nothing is lacking and nothing is in excess." If we can stand in the place where there is no sense of anything lacking or anything being completed, we do not give in to the anxiety of perfection or nonperfection.

Lombardo translates this line as "When you see things like this, how can you be incomplete?" As we have discussed earlier, incompleteness or *dukkha* is a relational quality obtained in the skewed perceptual imperatives of the observer. Once the lens of perception has been cleansed, and we can see that one contains the many, and many contain the One—so how can there be separation and a sense of incompleteness?

To live in this faith is the road to nonduality, because the nondual is one with the trusting mind:

Lombardo translates this line as, "Trust and Mind are not two; Not-two is *Trust in Mind*." Dunn and Jourdan have a more poetic translation: "To live and trust in the nondual mind is to move with true freedom, to live without anxiety, upon the Great Way." As mentioned earlier, translating *xin* or *hsin* as faith is always problematic in European languages, for the understanding of "faith" gets conflated with the general assumptions of Judeo-Christian traditions. "Trust" or "trusting" is a more accurate rendering of *hsin*; this trust is a trust in the experience of equanimity when all distinctions have been let go, when the nondual mode of perception is the primary condition of existence. One Mind is continually unfolding itself as being-in-becoming, and it trusts *itself* as that process. In that sense trust itself is the One Mind, and One Mind itself is trust.

Words! The Way is beyond language:

Even before Nagarjuna, in India, and Sengchao in China had created a dialectic for deconstructing linguistic categories, Zhuangzi was parodying the logicians:

> Take the case of some words. I do not know which of them are in any way connected with reality or which are not at all connected with reality. If some that are so connected and some that are not so connected are connected with one another, then as regards truth or falsehood the former cease to be in any way different from the latter. However, just as an experiment, I will now say them: "If there was a beginning, there must have been a time before the beginning began, and if there was a time before the beginning began, there must have been a time before the time before the beginning began. If there is being, there must also be not-being. If there was a time before there began to be any not-being, there must also have been a time before the time before there began to be any not-being. But here am I, talking about being and not-being and still do not know whether it is being that exists and not-being that does not exist, or being that does not exist and not-being that really exists! I have spoken, and do not know whether I have said something that means anything or said nothing that has any meaning at all."[62]

One Mind and its functioning are beyond words and language. Bodhidharma, the personage in whom Chan finds its root, famously summarized his teaching as: "Without depending on words and letters, pointing directly to one's own mind, realizing Buddha-nature," and all Zen teachers since his time have continued to point out that cultivation and realization of the Great Way is not dependent on words and verbal understanding.

For in it there is no yesterday, no tomorrow, no today:

Just as the Way is beyond language it is also beyond psychological time. The Way continues to unfold in its own timelessness rather than being confined

to a temporal framework. We now know from physics that "time" does not
exist outside of human reckoning. The Way or the Tao or the Dharma
equally does not depend on human reckoning to be valid, just as the law of
gravity does not depend on human reckoning. A careful use of the conven-
tional language will encourage us to think in terms of the always-now rather
than the artificial constructs of yesterday, tomorrow, or today.

In the Bhaddekaratta Sutta of the Pali tripitaka, the Buddha said:

> For the past has been left behind,
> And the future has not been reached.
> Instead with insight let him see
> Each presently arisen state;
> Let him know that and be sure of it,
> Invincibly, unshakably.
> Today the effort must be made.[63]

In the lines above the emphasis is on the effort to be made in the always-
now rather than "today" as a temporal unit. There are only the ten thousand
things of the world unfolding themselves in the Great Way of the always-
now. This is the still point of the turning world. It is beyond belief, beyond
expression, beyond space, beyond time. Words fail to capture its depth and
clarity but its cultivation continues for those who care to cultivate it.

For the Buddha, "awakening" means to wake up from the dream-world
we live in. The freedom he spoke of is freedom from the prison of concep-
tualized thinking through which we live our lives. The freedom that Sengcan
seeks in his poem is always in the here and now rather than in some linguis-
tic or metaphysical abstraction. *Trust in Mind* is a message about being in the
world of the here-now rather than being caught hopelessly in conceptuality.
When one transcends all imperatives of longing-clinging-becoming, life and
death flow into each other like water and ice; being and living are not differ-
entiated from each other; being and becoming do not become needless con-
ceptual conflicts; life and living do not become conflicting metaphysical
abstractions. The Buddha taught that each moment is a moment of freedom.
Chan and Taoists added that each moment is complete as it is. If we make
peace with how each moment is unfolding, we enter the realm of One Mind.
Sengcan lived and died this way; any number of mystics and Zen masters have
lived and died this way. Is there any other way?

⊰≪ Appendix I ≫⊱

THESE DIFFERENT TRANSLATIONS of Sengcan's poem are offered to the interested reader with the intention of showing wide variations in translating from Chinese into English, in a wide range of poetic and literary expressions. In a certain way, these translations tell us more about the authors/translators themselves than the verse in question. Each translator, it would seem, is trying to find a certain coherence in how the archaic Chinese words speak to him. Each translation thus has a different idiom, a different rhythm, a different sensibility. I find that when I read these translations side by side, new insights and depths of the meaning reveal themselves to me. In the main text of this book, I have used the Richard Clarke translation for the purposes of this commentary, but it may be that other translations offer a more nuanced understanding of certain lines.

In their translation, Dunn and Jourdan have moved some of the lines out of their usual Chinese sequence to have a more poetic and free-flowing narrative. I have restored these lines back into the sequence simply to make the line by line translation easy for the reader to see. The reader should know that in the original Chinese these lines are not arranged into quatrains. It is possible to arrange them into thirty-six quatrains of four lines each as some of the translators have done but it is an artificial imposition on the original structure of the text. For ease of comparison I have imposed further on this arrangement by trying to present all the translations here in thirty-six quatrains even when the translator may not have intended it to be so arranged.

1. FAITH IN MIND
Clarke translation

The Great Way is not difficult
for those who have no preferences.
When love and hate are both absent
everything becomes clear and undisguised.

Make the smallest distinction, however,
and heaven and earth are set infinitely apart.
If you wish to see the truth
then hold no opinions for or against anything.

To set up what you like against what you dislike
is the disease of the mind.
When the deep meaning of things is not understood
the mind's essential [stillness] is disturbed to no avail.

The Way is perfect like vast space
where nothing is lacking and nothing is in excess.
Indeed, it is due to our choosing to accept or reject
that we do not see the true nature of things.

Live neither in the entanglements of outer things,
nor in inner feelings of emptiness.
Be serene in the Oneness of things
and such erroneous views will disappear by themselves.

2. INSCRIBED ON THE BELIEVING MIND
Suzuki translation

The Perfect Way knows no difficulties
Except that it refuses to make preference:
Only when freed from hate and love,
It reveals itself fully and without disguise.

A tenth of an inch's difference,
And heaven and earth are set apart:
If you want to see it manifest,
Take no thought either for or against it.

To set up what you like against what you dislike—
This is the disease of the mind:
When the deep meaning [of the Way] is not understood
Peace of mind is disturbed and nothing is gained.

[The Way] is perfect like unto vast space,
With nothing wanting, nothing superfluous:
It is indeed due to making choice
That its suchness is lost sight of.

Pursue not the outer entanglements,
Dwell not in the inner void;
When the mind rests serene in the oneness of things,
The dualism vanishes by itself.

3. ON TRUST IN THE HEART
Waley translation

The Perfect Way is only difficult
for those who pick and choose;
Do not like, do not dislike,
all will then be clear.

Make a hairbreadth difference,
and Heaven and Earth are set apart;
If you want the truth to stand clear before you,
never be for or against.

The struggle between "for" and "against"
is the mind's worst disease;
While the deep meaning is misunderstood,
it is useless to meditate on Rest.

It is blank and featureless as space;
it has no "too little" or "too much;"
Only because we take and reject
does it seem to us not to be so.

Do not chase after Entanglements as though they were real things,
Do not try to drive pain away by pretending that it is not real;
Pain, if you seek serenity in Oneness,
will vanish of its own accord.

4. THE BELIEVING MIND
Blyth translation

There is nothing difficult about the Great Way,
but, avoid choosing.
Only when you neither love nor hate
does it appear in all clarity.

A hair's breadth of deviation from it,
and a deep gulf is set between heaven and earth.
If you want to get hold of what it looks like,
do not be anti- or pro- anything.

The conflict of longing and loathing—
this is the disease of the mind.
Not knowing the profound meaning of things,
we disturb our [original] peace of mind to no purpose.

Perfect like Great Space,
The Way has nothing lacking, nothing in excess.
Truly, because of our accepting and rejecting,
we have not the suchness of things.

Neither follow after,
nor dwell with the Doctrine of the Void
If the mind is at peace,
these wrong views disappear of themselves.

5. HAVE FAITH IN YOUR MIND
Lu translation

It is not hard to realize your Mind
Which should not be an object of your choice.
Throw like and dislike away
And you'll be clear about it.

The slightest deviation from it means
A gulf as deep as that 'twixt heaven and earth.
If you want it to manifest
Be not for or against a thing.

For that is contentious,
A disease of the mind.
If its profoundness you ignore
You can never practice stillness.

Perfect like the great void it lacks
Nothing and has naught in excess.
If you discriminate
You will miss its suchness.

To external causes cling not, stay
Not in the void (that is relative),
If you can be impartial
Differentiation ceases.

6. THE BELIEVING MIND
Sheng-yen translation

The Supreme Way is not difficult
If only you do not pick and choose.
Neither love nor hate,
And you will clearly understand.

Be off by a hair,
And you are as far apart as heaven from earth.
If you want it to appear,
Be neither for nor against.

For and against opposing each other—
This is the mind's disease.
Without recognizing the mysterious principle
It is useless to practice quietude.

The Way is perfect like great space,
Without lack, without excess.
Because of grasping and rejecting,
You cannot attain it.

Do not pursue conditioned existence;
Do not abide in acceptance of emptiness.
In oneness and equality,
Confusion vanishes of itself.

7. INSCRIPTION ON FAITH IN MIND
By Dusan Pajin

The best way is not difficult
It only excludes picking and choosing
Once you stop loving and hating
It will enlighten itself.

Depart for a hairbreadth
And heaven and earth are set apart,
If you want it to appear
Do not be for or against.

To set longing against loathing
Makes the mind sick,
Not knowing the deep meaning (of the way)
It is useless to quiet thoughts.

Complete it is like great vacuity
With nothing lacking, nothing in excess.
When you grasp and reject
There is no suchness.

Do not follow conditions,
Do not dwell in emptiness.
Cherishing oneness in the hearth,
Everything will stop by itself.

8. TRUST IN MIND
Lombardo translation

The Great Way is not difficult:
Just have no preferences.
Cut off all likes and dislikes
And it is clear like space.

The slightest distinction
Splits heaven from earth.
To see the truth
Don't be for or against.

Likes and dislikes
Are the mind's disease.
If you miss the deep meaning,
Stilling your thoughts is of no use.

It is like vast space,
Nothing missing, nothing extra.
If you choose or reject,
You cannot see things as they are.

Outside, don't get tangled in things.
Inside, don't get lost in emptiness.
Be still and become One,
And it all stops by itself.

9. A SONG OF ENLIGHTENMENT
Dunn and Jourdan translation

The Great Way is effortless
for those who live in choiceless awareness.
To choose without preference
is to be clear.

Even the slightest personal preference
and your whole world becomes deluded.
To perceive reality as it is
is to live with an open mind.

When the lens you look through
reflects your personal bias,
your view of reality is clouded.
Truth simply is.
The clouded mind cannot know it.

The Great Way is empty—
like a vast sky.
Silence the busy mind
and know this perfection.

Be seduced neither by the outer world
nor by your inner emptiness.
Reside in the oneness of things
where distinctions are meaningless.

10. GATHA OF SENG T'SAN
Zen Buddhist Order of Hsu Yun translation

It's not difficult to discover your Buddha Mind
But just don't try to search for it.
Cease accepting and rejecting possible places
Where you think it can be found
And it will appear before you.

Be warned! The slightest exercise of preference
Will open a gulf as wide and deep
as the space between heaven and earth.
If you want to encounter your Buddha Mind
Don't have opinions about anything.

Opinions produce argument
And contentiousness is a disease of the mind.
Plunge into the depths.
Stillness is deep. There's nothing profound in shallow waters.

The Buddha Mind is perfect and it encompasses the universe.
It lacks nothing and has nothing in excess.
If you think that you can choose between its parts
You'll miss its very essence.

Don't cling to externals, the opposite things,
the things that exist as relative.
Accept them all impartially
And you won't have to waste time in pointless choosing.

And when oneness is not thoroughly understood,
In two ways loss is sustained—
The denial of reality may lead to its absolute negation,
While the upholding of the void may result in contradicting itself.

Wordiness and intellection—
The more with them the further astray we go;
Away therefore with wordiness and intellection,
And there is no place where we cannot pass freely.

When we return to the root, we gain the meaning;
When we pursue the external objects, we lose the reason.
The moment we are enlightened within,
We go beyond the voidness of a world confronting us,
Transformations going on in an empty world which confronts us,
Appear real because of Ignorance.

Try not to seek after the true,
Only cease to cherish opinions.
Tarry not with dualism,
Carefully avoid pursuing it.

When you try to stop activity to achieve passivity
your very effort fills you with activity.
As long as you remain in one extreme or the other
you will never know Oneness.

Those who do not live in the single Way
fail in both activity and passivity, assertion and denial.
To deny the reality of things is to miss their reality;
to assert the emptiness of things is to miss their reality.

The more you talk and think about it,
the further astray you wander from the truth.
Stop talking and thinking, and there is nothing you will
    not be able to know.

To return to the root is to find the meaning,
but to pursue appearances is to miss the source.
At the moment of inner enlightenment
there is a going beyond appearance and emptiness.
The changes that appear to occur in the empty world
we call real only because of our ignorance.

Do not search for the truth;
only cease to cherish opinions.
Do not remain in the dualistic state;
avoid such pursuits carefully.

3. Waley-2

Stop all movement in order to get rest,
and rest will itself be restless;
Linger over either extreme,
and Oneness is forever lost.

Those who cannot attain to Oneness in either case will fail:
To banish Reality is to sink deeper into the Real;
Allegiance to the Void implies denial of its voidness.

The more you talk about it, the more you think about it,
the further from it you go;
Stop talking, stop thinking,
and there is nothing you will not understand.

Return to the Root and you will find the Meaning;
Pursue the Light, and you will lose its source,
Look inward, and in a flash
you will conquer the Apparent and the Void.
For the whirligigs of Apparent and Void
all come from mistaken views.

There is no need to seek Truth;
only stop having views.
Do not accept either position,
examine it or pursue it.

4. Blyth-2

When activity is stopped and there is passivity,
this passivity again is a state of activity.
Remaining in movement or quiescence,
how shall you know the One?

Not thoroughly understanding the unity of the Way,
both (activity and quiescence) are failures.
If you get rid of phenomena, all things are lost:
If you follow after the void, you turn your back on
the self-lessness of things.

The more talking and thinking,
the farther from the truth.
Cutting off all speech, all thought,
there is nowhere that you cannot go.

Returning to the root, we get the essence;
Following after appearances we lose the spirit.
If only for a moment we see within,
we have surpassed the emptiness of things.
Changes that go on in this emptiness
all arise because of our ignorance.

Do not seek for the Truth,
only stop having an opinion.
Do not remain in the relative view of things;
religiously avoid following it.

To stop disturbance leads to stillness
Which, if clung to, stirs the mind. But if
To opposites you cling
How can you know the One?

If you do not recognize One Mind
Two opposites will lead you nowhere.
To avoid what is means to cling to what is not,
To cling to what is not means to revive what is.

The more you talk and think,
The further you are from it.
If you can halt all speech and thought
You will find it everywhere.

If you think success means to return
all things to their source,
You will differ (from our Sect)
by clinging to its function.

The moment you look within
You surpass your contemplation
Of the void which is always changing
Due to your discriminating views.

Do not seek the real
But your false views lay down.
Avoid the real and the false
And never search for either.

5. *Lu*-2

Stop activity and return to stillness,
And that stillness will be even more active.
Only stagnating in duality,
How can you recognize oneness?

If you fail to penetrate oneness,
Both places lose their function.
Banish existence and you fall into existence;
Follow emptiness and you turn your back on it.

Excessive talking and thinking
Turn you from harmony with the Way.
Cut off thinking and talking,
And there is nowhere you cannot penetrate.

Return to the root and attain the principle;
Pursue illumination and you lose it.

6. *Sheng-yen*-2

One moment of reversing the light
Is greater than the previous emptiness.
The previous emptiness is transformed;
It was all a product of deluded views.

No need to see the real;
Just extinguish your views.
Do not abide in dualistic views;
Take care not to seek after them.

Rest to stop motion,
And rest will move you again.
If you are merely in either,
How will you know oneness?

Not understanding oneness
You will miss in two ways.
Expelling being you will be without it,
Following emptiness you are always behind it.

The more words and thoughts
The more you will go astray
Stop speaking, stop thinking
And there is nothing you cannot understand.

Return to the root and obtain the purport.
Following the outcome you lose the source.
For a moment turn inward,
And surpass the emptiness of things.
Changes that go on in emptiness
All have their cause in ignorance.

Do not seek the true,
Only abstain from views.
Do not dwell in dual views,
Be careful not to pursue them.

7. *Pajin*-2

Stop moving to become still
And the stillness will move.
If you hold on to opposites,
How can you understand One?

If you don't understand One,
This and that cannot function.
Denied, the world goes on.
Pursued, emptiness is lost.

The more you think and talk,
The more you lose the Way.
Cut off all thinking
And pass freely anywhere.

Return to the root and get the drift,
Chase outcomes and lose the source.
One clear moment within
Illumines the emptiness before you.
Emptiness changing into things
Is only our deluded view.

Do not seek the truth,
Only put down your opinions.
Do not live in the world of opposites.
Be careful! Never go that way.

8. *Lombardo*-2

9. Dunn & Jourdan-2

Trying to still the mind
inhibits the experience of oneness,
for the very action of trying
is the busy mind at work.

Live in the Great Way
where action is stillness and silence pervades.
Deny the reality of things
and miss true nature.
Assert that emptiness exists
and it will disappear.

To experience reality,
stop using words;
for the more you talk about things
the farther away from the truth you stray.

Return to oneness and discover the essence.
Being dazzled by appearance you miss the truth.
Go beyond both appearance and emptiness
and find the unmoving center.
Pursue the confusion of your opinions
and the eternal mind is lost.

10. Hsu Yun-2

Judgments and discriminations block the flow
and stir the passions.
They roil the mind that needs stillness and peace.

If you go from either-or, this and that,
or any of the countless opposites,
You'll miss the whole, the One.
Following an opposite you'll be led astray,
away from the balancing center.
How can you hope to gain the One?
To decide what is, is to determine what's not.
But determining what's not can occupy you
so that it becomes what is.

The more you talk and think
the farther away you get.
Cease talking and thinking
and you'll find it everywhere.

If you let all things return to their source, that's fine.
But if you stop to think that this is your goal
And that this is what success depends upon
And strive and strive instead of simply letting go,
You won't be doing Zen.
The moment that you start discriminating and preferring
you miss the mark.

As soon as you have right and wrong,
Confusion enters, the mind is lost.
The two exist because of the one,
But hold not even to this one.

When the one mind is not disturbed,
The ten thousand things offer no offense.
When no offence is offered by them, they are as if not existing;
When the mind is not disturbed, it is as if there is no mind.

The subject is quieted as the object ceases,
The object ceases as the subject is quieted.
The object is an object for the subject,
The subject is a subject for an object.

Know that the relativity of the two
Rests ultimately on the oneness of the Void.
In the oneness of the void the two are one,
And each of the two contains in itself all the ten thousand things.

When no discrimination is made between this and that,
How can a one-sided and prejudiced view arise?
The Great Way is calm and large-minded,
Nothing is easy, nothing is hard.

If there is even a trace of this and that, of right and wrong,
the Mind-essence will be lost in confusion.
Although all dualities come from the One,
do not be attached even to this One.

When the mind exists undisturbed in the Way
nothing in the world can offend,
and when a thing can no longer offend,
it ceases to exist in the old way.
When no discriminating thoughts arise,
the old mind ceases to exist.

When thought objects vanish, the thinking subject vanishes,
as when the mind vanishes, objects vanish.
Things are objects because of the subject [mind];
the mind [subject] is such because of things [object].

Understand the relativity of these two
and the basic reality: the unity of emptiness.
In this Emptiness the two are indistinguishable
and each contains in itself the whole world.

If you do not discriminate between coarse and fine
you will not be tempted to prejudice and opinion.
To live in the Great Way is neither easy nor difficult.

3. *Waley-3*

At the least thought of "Is" and "Isn't"
There is chaos and the Mind is lost.
Though the two exist because of the One.
do not cling to the One;

Only when no thought arises
are the Dharmas without blame.
No blame, no Dharmas;
no arising, no thought.

The doer vanishes along with the deed,
The deed disappears when the doer is annihilated.
The deed has no function apart from the doer;
The doer has no function apart from the deed.

The ultimate Truth about both Extremes is
that they are One Void.
In that One Void the two are not distinguished;
Each contains complete within itself the Ten Thousand Forms.

Only if we boggle over fine and coarse
are we tempted to take sides.
In its essence the Great Way is all-embracing;
It is as wrong to call it easy as to call it hard.

Partial views are irresolute and insecure,
Now at a gallop, now lagging in the rear.

4. *Blyth-3*

If there's the slightest trace of this and that,
the Mind is lost in a maze of complexity.
Duality arises from unity;
but do not be attached to this unity.

When the Mind is One, and nothing happens,
everything in the world is unblameable.
If things are unblamed, they cease to exist;
If nothing happens, there is no mind.

When things cease to exist, the mind follows them:
When the mind vanishes, things also follow it.
Things are things because of the mind;
the Mind is the Mind because of things.

If you wish to know what these two are,
they are originally one Emptiness.
In this Void, both (Mind and things) are one,
all the myriad phenomena contained in both.

If you do not distinguish "refined" and "coarse,"
how can you be *for* this and *against* that?
The activity of the Great Way is vast;
it is neither easy nor difficult.

Small views are full of foxy fears;
the faster the slower.

5. Lu-3

Once you start to choose between what's right and wrong,
You will become confused and lose your Mind.
All pairs from the One Mind spring
Which never should be clung to.

If the One Mind does not stir
Then all things will be harmless.
Things that are harmless cease to be,
Mind that stirs but does not exist.

Subjects disengaged from objects vanish,
Objects like their creator disappear.
Objects are caused by subjects
On whose existence they depend.

If you would understand dualities
Know that they spring from Voidness absolute.
The absolute and all dualities
Are one, from it all things originate.

When you cease choosing between the coarse
And fine all prejudices die.
Since the Great Mind embraces all,
To realize it is not difficult
Or easy.

In their distrust the ignorant
Waver between eagerness and hesitation.

6. Sheng-yen-3

As soon as there is right and wrong
The mind is scattered and lost.
Two comes from one,
Yet do not even keep the one.

When one mind does not arise,
Myriad dharmas are without defect.
Without defect, without dharmas,
No arising, no mind.

The subject is extinguished with the object.
The object sinks away with the subject.
Object is object because of the subject;
Subject is subject because of the object.

Know that the two
Are originally one emptiness.
In one emptiness the two are the same,
Containing all phenomena.

Not seeing fine or coarse,
How can there be any bias?
The Great Way is broad,
Neither easy nor difficult.

With narrow views and doubts,
Haste will slow you down.

The slightest trace of right and wrong
And mind is lost in confusion.
One being is the source of the two
However, do not even maintain the one.

With one mind there is no arising,
Then everything is without blame.
No blame, no things.
No arising, no mind.

The subject follows when the object ceases
The object is expelled when the subject sinks.
The object is related to the subject
The subject is related to the object.

If you want to know these two
Their origin is one emptiness.
In one emptiness both are equal
Evenly containing innumerable forms.

Do not differentiate coarse and fine
And you will not be for or against.
The great way is allembracing
Neither easy nor difficult.

Small views are irresolute, full of doubt,
Now in haste, then too late.
Grasp beyond measure
And you will go astray.

If you make right and wrong,
Your mind is lost in confusion.
Two comes from One,
But do not cling even to One.

If one mind does not arise,
The ten thousand things are without fault.
No fault, no things,
No arising, no mind.

This comes when that goes.
That rises when this sinks.

Understand both
As originally one emptiness.
In emptiness the two are the same,
And each holds the ten thousand things.

If you do not see coarse or fine,
How can you prefer one to the other?
The Way is calm and wide,
Not easy, not difficult.

But small minds get lost.
Hurrying, they fall behind.
Clinging, they go too far,
Sure to take a wrong turn.

Rather than focus on knowing the truth
simply cease to be seduced by your opinions.
Duality appears in minutest traces;
carefully avoid the trap.

If there is even an inkling of right or wrong
the enlightened mind ceases to be.
Everything there is comes from oneness
but oneness cannot be described.
Holding any trace of it in the mind
is to deny the essence of emptiness.

When the mind is still,
nothing can disturb it.
When nothing can disturb it,
reality ceases to exist in the old way.

When you understand the relationship of subject and object,
thinker and thought—
and how they create each other—
you recognize that these are not two, but one.

Don't strive to know particulars
when what you want to experience is one.
It is beyond the nature of the mind to perceive
the reality it cannot describe.

Seeking the real is a false view
which should also be abandoned.
Just let go. Cease searching and choosing.
Decisions give rise to confusions
and in confusion where can a mind go?

All the opposing pairs come from the One Great Buddha Mind.
Accept the pairs with gentle resignation.

The Buddha Mind stays calm and still,
Keep your mind within it and nothing can disturb you.
The harmless and the harmful cease to exist.

Subjects when disengaged from their objects vanish
Just as surely as objects,
when disengaged from their subjects, vanish too.
Each depends on the existence of the other.

Understand this duality and you'll see
that both issue from the Void of the Absolute.
The Ground of all Being contains all the opposites.
From the One, all things originate.

1. *Clarke-4*

But those with limited views are fearful and irresolute:
the faster they hurry, the slower they go,
and clinging [attachment] cannot be limited;
even to be attached to the idea of enlightenment is to go astray.

Just let things be in their own way,
and there will be neither coming nor going.
Obey the nature of things [your own nature],
and you will walk freely and undisturbed.

When thought is in bondage the truth is hidden,
for everything is murky and unclear,
and the burdensome practice of judging brings annoyance and weariness.
What benefit can be derived from distinctions and separations?

If you wish to move in the One Way
do not dislike even the world of senses and ideas.
Indeed, to accept them fully is identical with true Enlightenment.

The wise man strives to no goals
but the foolish man fetters himself.
There is one Dharma, not many;
distinctions arise from the clinging needs of the ignorant.

To seek Mind with the mind is the greatest of all mistakes.
Rest and unrest derive from illusion;
with enlightenment there is no liking and disliking.

2. *Suzuki-4*

Small views are irresolute,
The more in haste the tardier they go.
Clinging never keeps itself within bounds,
It is sure to go in the wrong way.

Let go loose, and things are as they may be,
While the essence neither departs nor abides.
Obey the nature of things, and you are in concord with the Way,
Calm and easy and free from annoyance.

But when your thoughts are tied, you turn away from the truth,
They grow heavier and duller and are not at all sound.
When they are not sound, the soul is troubled;
What is the use of being partial and one-sided then?

If you want to walk the course of the One Vehicle,
Be not prejudiced against the six sense-objects.
When you are not prejudiced against the six sense-objects,
You in turn identify yourself with Enlightenment.

The wise are non-active,
While the ignorant bind themselves up;
While in the Dharma itself there is no individuation,
They ignorantly attach themselves to particular objects.

It is their own minds that create illusions—
Is it not the greatest of self-contradictions?
Ignorance begets the dualism of rest and unrest,
The enlightened have no likes and dislikes.

Clinging to this or to that beyond measure
The heart trusts to bypaths that lead it astray.

Let things take their own course;
knowing that the Essence will neither go nor stay;
Let your nature blend with the Way
and wander in it free from care.

Thoughts that are fettered turn from Truth,
Sink into unwise habit of "not liking."
"Not liking" brings weariness of spirit;
estrangements serve no purpose.

If you want to follow the doctrine of the One,
do not rage against the World of the Senses.
Only by accepting the World of the Senses
can you share in the True Perception.

Those who know most, do least;
folly ties its own bonds.
In the Dharma there are no separate dharmas,
only the foolish cleave to their own preferences and attachments.

To use Thought to devise thoughts,
what more misguided than this?
Ignorance creates Rest and Unrest;
Wisdom neither loves nor hates.

3. Waley-4

When we attach ourselves to this [idea of enlightenment],
we lose our balance: we infallibly enter the crooked way.

When we are not attached to anything,
all things are just as they are.
With activity, there is no going, no staying.
Obeying our nature, we are in accord with the Way,
Wandering freely, without annoyance.

When our thinking is tied, it turns from the truth;
it is dark, submerged, wrong.
It is foolish to irritate your mind;
why shun this and be friends with that?

If you wish to travel in the True Vehicle,
do not dislike the Six Dusts.
Indeed, not hating the Six Dusts
is identical with Real Enlightement.

The wise man does nothing;
the fool shackles himself.
The Truth has no distinctions;
these come from our foolish clinging to this or that.

Seeking the Mind with the mind—
is not this the greatest of all mistakes?
Illusion produces rest and motion;
illumination destroys liking and disliking.

4. Blyth-4

If you grasp at it, you will be in the wrong
Falling into the way of the heretics.

If you lay it down
It stays not nor goes.
With the Tao unite your nature
And you will be free from troubles.

Clinging from the real strays
And to confusion leads.
Discrimination's useless
So weary not your mind.

If you want to know the One
Reject not six sense data.
If they're not rejected
They are one with Bodhi.

The wise man is non-active,
The ignorant bind themselves.
All things are the same at heart
But clinging's from delusion.

If the mind is used to seek itself,
Is this not a grave mistake?
Delusion brings stillness and disturbance;
Bodhi is far beyond all good and evil.

Attach to it and you lose the measure;
The mind will enter a deviant path.

Let it go and be spontaneous,
Experience no going or staying.
Accord with your nature, unite with the Way,
Wander at ease, without vexation.

Bound by thoughts, you depart from the real;
And sinking into a stupor is as bad.
It is not good to weary the spirit.
Why alternate between aversion and affection?

If you wish to enter the one vehicle,
Do not be repelled by the sense realm.
With no aversion to the sense realm,
You become one with true enlightenment.

The wise have no motives;
Fools put themselves in bondage.
One dharma is not different from another.
The deluded mind clings to whatever it desires.

Using mind to cultivate mind—
Is this not a great mistake?
The erring mind begets tranquility and confusion;
In enlightenment there are no likes or dislikes.

7. Pajin-4

Letting go leads to spontaneity,
Essence neither goes nor abides.
Accord your nature with the way
And go free of troubles.

Fettered thinking strays from the real,
It darkens, sinks and spoils.
To weary the spirit is not good.
Of what use are strange and familiar?

In following the One vehicle,
Do not dislike the six sense objects.
Not disliking the six sense objects
Turns out equal to perfect awakenness.

The wise performs through nonaction.
The fool ties himself.
Things are not different,
Ignorance leads to preference.

To use the mind to hold the mind
Is it not a great mistake?
Out of confusion arise rest and disturbance.
Awakening negates liking and disliking.

All opposite sides
Lead to absurd consideration.

8. Lombardo-4

Just let it be! In the end,
Nothing goes, nothing stays.
Follow nature and find the Way,
Free, easy, and undisturbed.

Tied to your thoughts, you lose the truth,
Become heavy, dull, and unwell.
Not well, the mind is troubled,
So why hold or reject anything?

To ride the One Vehicle,
Do not despise the six senses.
Not despising the six senses
Is already enlightenment.

The wise do not act,
The ignorant bind themselves.
In true Dharma there is no this or that,
So why blindly chase desires?

Using mind to grasp mind
Is the original mistake.
Peaceful and troubled are only ideas.
Enlightenment has no likes or dislikes.

All opposites arise
From faulty views.

Oneness has nothing to do with hard or easy
for it is beyond every opposite.
It cannot be found, it cannot be retained.
To grasp at it is to miss it entirely.

Not trying to go faster or slower,
be still, and let go.
Just let things be
for it is exactly as it should be.

Returning to your true nature,
spontaneity and essence are found.
This is the space that always exists
and that holds all within.

True reality is hidden by the practice of thought
but also in the denial.
Accept the reality of not naming things
and rest in the silence of being.

Use your senses to experience reality,
for they are part of your empty mind.
This empty mind takes note of all it perceives
and is guided by its sensing needs.

While the ignorant are bound to emotional choices—
attaching themselves to their ignorance,
the wise experience life through not reacting at all—
unswayed, uninvolved, unattached.

9. *Dunn & Jourdan-4*

What a waste of time to choose between coarse and fine.
Since the Great Mind gives birth to all things,
Embrace them all and let your prejudices die.
To realize the Great Mind be neither hesitant nor eager.

If you try to grasp it, you'll cling to air
and fall into the way of heretics.

10. *Hsu Yun-4*

Where is the Great Dao? Can you lay It down?
Will It stay or go?
Is It not everywhere waiting for you
to unite your nature with Its nature
and become as trouble free as It is?

Don't tire your mind by worrying about what is real
and what isn't,
About what to accept and what to reject.

If you want to know the One,
let your senses experience what comes your way,
But don't be swayed and don't involve yourself in what comes.

The wise man acts without emotion
and seems not to be acting at all.
The ignorant man lets his emotions get involved.
The wise man knows that all things are part of the One.
The ignorant man sees differences everywhere.

All dualities come from ignorant inference.
The are like dreams or flowers in air:
foolish to try to grasp them.

Gain and loss, right and wrong:
such thoughts must finally be abolished at once.
If the eye never sleeps, all dreams will naturally cease.

If the mind makes no discriminations,
the ten thousand things are as they are, of single essence.
To understand the mystery of this One-essence
is to be released from all entanglements.

When all things are seen equally
the timeless Self-essence is reached.
No comparisons or analogies are possible
in this causeless, relationless state.

Consider movement stationary and the stationary in motion,
both movement and rest disappear.
When such dualities cease to exist Oneness itself cannot exist.

1. *Clarke-5*

All forms of dualism
Are ignorantly contrived by the mind itself.
They are like unto visions and flowers in the air:
Why should we trouble ourselves to take hold of them?

2. *Suzuki-5*

Gain and loss, right and wrong—
Away with them once for all!
If an eye never falls asleep,
All dreams by themselves cease.

If the mind retains its oneness,
The ten thousand things are of one suchness.
When the deep mystery of one suchness is fathomed,
All of a sudden we forget the external entanglements.

When the ten thousand things are viewed in their oneness,
We return to the origin and remain what we are.
Forget the wherefore of things,
And we attain to a state beyond analogy.

Movement stopped is no movement,
And rest set in motion is no rest.
When dualism does no more obtain,
Even oneness itself remains not as such.

3. Waley-5

All that belongs to the Two Extremes
is inference falsely drawn.
A dream-phantom, a flower in the air.
Why strive to grasp it in the hand?

"Is" and "Isn't," gain and loss
banish one for all.
If the eyes do not close in sleep
there can be no evil dreams.

If the mind makes no distinctions
all Dharmas become one.
Let the One with its mystery blot out
all memory of complications.

Let the thought of the Dharmas as All-One
bring you to the So-in-itself.
Thus their origin is forgotten and nothing is left
to make us pit one against the other.

Regard motion as thought it were stationary,
and what becomes of motion?
Treat the stationary as thought it moved,
and that disposes of the stationary.
Both these having been disposed of,
what becomes of the One?

4. Blyth-5

All these pairs of opposites
are created by our own folly.
Dreams, delusions, flowers of air—
why should we be so anxious to have them in our grasp?

Profit and loss, right and wrong—
away with them once for all!
If the eye does not sleep,
all dreaming ceases naturally.

If the mind makes no discriminations,
all things are as they really are.
In the deep mystery of this "things as they are,"
we are release from our relations to them.

When all things are seen "with equal mind"
they return to their nature.
No description by analogy if possible
of this state where all relations have ceased.

When we stop movement, there is no-movement.
When we stop resting, there is no-rest.
When both cease to be,
how can Unity subsist?

The duality of all things
Issues from false discriminations.
A dream, an illusion, a flower in the sky—
How could they be worth grasping?

Gain and loss, right and wrong—
Discard them all at once.
If the eyes do not close in sleep,
All dreams will cease of themselves.

If the mind does not discriminate,
All dharmas are of one suchness.
The essence of one suchness is profound;
Unmoving, conditioned things are forgotten.

Contemplate all dharmas as equal,
And you return to things as they are.
When the subject disappears,
There can be no measuring or comparing.

Stop activity and there is no activity;
When activity stops, there is no rest.
Since two cannot be established,
How can there be one?

In the very ultimate,
Rules and standards do not exist.

6. *Sheng-yen-5*

And the pair of opposites
From discrimination come.
Dreams, illusions and flowers in
The sky are not worth attachment.

Gain and loss, and right and wrong
Should be laid down now at once.
If your eyes close not in sleep
All your dreams will disappear.

If you do not discriminate,
Then all things will be as they are.
Profound is this state of suchness,
Lofty and beyond illusions.

If things are not thought different,
To their nature they will return.
When they disappear,
Mind's without compare.

When it stops moving disturbance is no more;
When all motion ceases, stillness also stops.
When opposites disappear,
Where then can the One Mind be?

When for the ultimate you search,
You find it has no pattern.

5. *Lu-5*

7. Pajin-5

Dreams, illusions, flowers in the air
Why strive to grasp them?

Profit and loss, right and wrong
Away with this once for all.
If the eyes are not closed
All dreams stop by themselves.

If the mind does not discriminate
All things are of one suchness.
In the deep essence of one suchness
Resolutely neglect conditions.

When all things are beheld as even
You return again to spontaneity.
Put an end to the cause
And nothing can be compared.

Cease movement and no movement arises.
Set rest in motion and there is no resting.
When both do not make a whole
How will one be for you?

Investigate to the end
And there is no principle or rule retained.
Accord the mind with Impartiality
Which stops every action.

8. Lombardo-5

Illusions, flowers in the air—
Why try to grasp them?

Win, lose, right, wrong—
Put it all down!
If the eye never sleeps
Dreams disappear by themselves.

If the mind makes no distinctions
The ten thousand things are one essence.
See the deep and dark essence
And be free from entanglements.

See the ten thousand things as equal
And return to your original nature.
Without any ground for distinctions
Comparisons are not possible.

Stop and there is no motion.
Move and there is no stillness.
Without motion or stillness
How can a single thing exist?

In true nature
There are no goals or plans.
In the mind before thinking
No effort is made.

The need to name, the need to distinguish
are born of a clinging fear.
Remain unattached to every thought
and know the true nature of being.

Be inattentive and mind is an irritant
with dreams that disturb reality.
Why look for trouble and distress
when awareness is so freeing?

High and low, good and bad—
all duality disappears,
and all dreams abate
when the inner calm is met.

When the mind ceases all movement,
ceases judging,
ceases conceptualizing,
the deep cool essence of suchness
becomes a way of life.

When all things are perceived
with an open mind,
they return to their natural way.

All things are the same at their core
but clinging to one and discarding another
Is living in illusion.
A mind is not a fit judge of itself.
It is prejudiced in its own favor or disfavor.
It cannot see anything objectively.

Bodhi is far beyond all notions of good and evil,
beyond all the pairs of opposites.
Daydreams are illusions and flowers in the sky never bloom.
They are figments of the imagination
and not worth your consideration.

Profit and Loss, right and wrong, coarse and fine.
Let them all go.
Stay awake. Keep your eyes open.
Your daydreams will disappear.

If you do not make judgments, everything will be
exactly as it is supposed to be.
Deep is the Tathagata's wisdom,
Lofty and beyond all illusions.

This is the One to which all things return
provided you do not separate them,
keeping some and casting others away.

1. *Clarke-6*

To this ultimate finality no law or description applies.
For the unified mind in accord with the Way
all self-centered striving ceases.

Doubts and irresolutions vanish and life in true faith is possible.
With a single stroke we are freed from bondage;
nothing clings to us and we hold to nothing.

All is empty, clear, self-illuminating,
with no exertion of the mind's power.
Here thought, feeling, knowledge,
and imagination are of no value.

In this world of Suchness there is neither self nor other-than-self.
To come directly into harmony with this reality
just simply say when doubt arises, 'Not two.'

In this "not two" nothing is separate,
nothing is excluded.
No matter when or where,
enlightenment means entering this truth.

2. *Suzuki-6*

The ultimate end of things where they cannot go any further,
Is not bound by rules and measures:
The mind in harmony [with the Way] is the principle of identity
In which we find all doings in a quiescent state.

Irresolutions are completely done away with,
And the right faith is restored to is native straightness;
Nothing is retained now,
Nothing is to be memorized.

All is void, lucid, and self-illuminating,
There is no strain, no exertion, no wasting of energy—
This is where thinking never attains,
This is where the imagination fails to measure.

In the higher realm of True Suchness
There is neither "other" nor "self":
When a direct identification is asked for,
We can only say, "Not Two."

In being not two all is the same,
All that is is compreheneded in it:
The wise in the ten quarters,
They all enter into this absolute faith.

Things are ultimately, in their finality,
subject to no law.
For the accordant mind in its unity,
[individual] activity ceases.

All doubts are cleared up,
True faith is confirmed.
Nothing remains behind;
there is not anything we must remember.

Empty, lucid, self-illuminated,
with no over-exertion of the power of the mind.
This where thought is useless,
this is what knowledge cannot fathom.

In the World of Reality,
there is no self, no other-than-self.
Should you desire immediate correspondence [with this Reality]
all that can be said is "No duality!"

When there is no duality, all things are one,
there is nothing that is not included.
The Enlightened of all times and places
have all entered into this Truth.

Truth cannot be increased or decreased;
an [instantaneous] thought lasts a myriad years.
There is no here, no there;
Infinity is before our eyes.

At the ultimate point, beyond which you can go no further,
You get to where there are no rules, no standards
To where thought can accept Impartiality,
To where effect of action ceases.

Doubt is washed away,
belief has no obstacle.
Nothing is left over, nothing remembered.

Space is bright, but self-illumined;
no power of mind is exerted.
Nor indeed could mere thought bring us to such a place.
Nor could sense or feeling comprehend it.

It is the Truly-so, the Transcendent Sphere,
where there is neither He nor I.
For swift converse with the sphere
use the concept "Not Two."

In the "Not Two" are no separate things,
yet all things are included.
The wise throughout the Ten Quarters
have had access to this Primal Truth.

For it is not a thing with extension in Time or Space;
A moment and an aeon for it are one.
Whether we see it or fail to see it,
it is manifest always and everywhere.

5. Lu-6

In this impartial mind
Duality has vanished.

When distrust ceases,
Your faith will be true.
When all is thrown away
There's nothing to remember.

The Mind that now is pure
Radiates and is not tired.
Since it is beyond discriminative thinking
It cannot be fathomed by that which knows and feels.

Such is the state absolute
Free from the self and others.
If you would be one with it
All duality avoid.

In all places the non-dual is
The same and there is naught outside it.
Sages everywhere
To this sect belong.

Which is beyond time, long or short,
For a thought lasts ten thousand years.
It neither is nor is not
For everywhere is here.

6. Sheng-yen-6

Develop a mind of equanimity,
And all deeds are put to rest.

Anxious doubts are completely cleared.
Right faith is made upright.
Nothing lingers behind,
Nothing can be remembered.

Bright and empty, functioning naturally,
The mind does not exert itself.
It is not a place of thinking,
Difficult for reason and emotion to fathom.

In the Dharma Realm of true suchness,
There is no other, no self.
To accord with it is vitally important;
Only refer to "not-two."

In not-two all things are in unity;
Nothing is not included.
The wise throughout the ten directions
All enter this principle.

This principle is neither hurried nor slow—
One thought for ten thousand years.
Abiding nowhere yet everywhere,
The ten directions are right before you.

All doubts are cleared
True faith is firm and harmonized.
Nothing is detained,
Nothing to remember.

Vacuous, enlightened, self-illumined,
Power of the mind is not exerted.
Thought is useless here,
Sense or feeling cannot fathom this.

In the real suchness of the thing realm
There is neither other nor self,
Swiftly to accord with that
Only express nonduality.

In nonduality all is equal,
Nothing is left out.
The wise from all directions
All belong to this teaching.

This teaching is not urgent, or extensive,
Beyond a moment, or an eon,
Not here, not there,
Everywhere in front of the eyes.

Very small and large are equal.
When boundaries are forgotten.

Doubts and worries disappear
When you see your true nature.
Nothing is left, nothing continues.

Bright emptiness shines by itself.
In the mind without effort
Thinking cannot take root.

In the true Dharma world
There is no self or other.
To enter this world
Just say "Not Two."

"Not two" includes everything,
Excludes nothing.
Enlightened beings everywhere
All enter this source.

This source is beyond time and space,
One moment, ten thousand years,
Not here, not anywhere,
Yet always before your eyes.

Infinitely small is infinitely large:
No boundaries, no differences.

Without any movement, without any description,
they are an undivided part of the whole.

True nature is impartial,
it has no causes or rules.
With the mind in undivided unity,
wisdom is radiated.

Trust in true nature,
keep your heart strong.
Pure mind is pure wisdom,
to part from it is foolish.

All is empty, all is clear,
no effort is made for none is needed.
When there is neither "self" nor "other,"
awareness simply is.

Meet doubt directly
with the words "not two"
and know that nothing can be separate and all is one.
There is nothing that is not included:
This is an eternal truth.

9. *Dunn & Jourdan-6*

Where can you put them anyway?
All things are within the One.
There is no outside.

The Ultimate has no pattern, no duality,
and is never partial.

10. *Hsu Yun-6*

Trust in this. Keep your faith strong.
When you lay down all distinctions there's nothing left
but Mind that is now pure, that radiates wisdom,
and is never tired.
When Mind passes beyond discriminations
Thoughts and feelings cannot plumb its depths.

The state is absolute and free.
There is neither self nor other.

You will be aware only that you are part of the One.
Everything is inside and nothing is outside.
All wise men everywhere understand this.

And this truth is beyond extension or diminution in time or space;
in it a single thought is ten thousand years.
Emptiness here, Emptiness there,
but the infinite universe stands always before your eyes.

Infinitely large and infinitely small:
no difference,
for definitions have vanished and no boundaries are seen.

So too with Being and non-Being.
Don't waste time in doubts and arguments
that have nothing to do with this.

One thing, all things:
move among and intermingle, without distinction.
To live in this realization is to be
without anxiety about non-perfection.

To live in this faith is the road to non-duality,
Because the non-dual is one with the trusting mind.
Words!
The Way is beyond language
for in it there is
no yesterday
no tomorrow
no today.

This absolute faith is beyond quickening [time] and extension [space].
One instant is ten thousand years;
No matter how things are conditioned, whether with "to be" or "not to be,"
It is manifest everywhere before you.

The infinitely small is as large as large can be,
When external conditions are forgotten;
The infinitely large is as small as small can be,
When objective limits are put out of sight.

What is is the same with what is not,
What is not is the same with what is:
Where this state of things fails to obtain,
Be sure not to tarry.

One in all,
All in one—
If only this is realized;
No more worry about your not being perfect!

The believing mind is not divided,
And undivided is the believing mind—
This is where words fail,
For it is not of the past, future, or present.

3. Waley-7

The very small is as the very large
when boundaries are forgotten;
The very large is as the very small
when its outlines are not seen.

Being is an aspect of Non-being;
Non-being is an aspect of Being.
In climes of thought where it is not so
the mind does ill to dwell.

The One is none other than the All,
the All none other than the One.
Take your stand on this,
and the rest will follow of its own accord.

To trust in the Heart is the Not-Two,
the Not-Two is to trust in the Heart.
I have spoken, but in vain;
for what can words tell
Of things that have no yesterday, tomorrow or today?

4. Blyth-7

The infinitely small is as large as the infinitely great;
for limits are non-existent here.
The infinitely large is as small as the infinitely minute;
No eye can see their boundaries.

What is, is not,
What is not, is.
Until you have grasped this fact,
your position is simply untenable.

One thing is all things;
All things are one thing.
If this is so for you,
there is no need to worry about perfect knowledge.

The believing mind is not dual;
what is dual is not the believing in mind.
Beyond all language,
for it there is no past, no present, no future.

The smallest equals the largest
For it is not confined by space.
The largest equals the smallest
For it is not within, without.

Is and is not are the same,
For what is not equals is.
If you cannot so awaken
Then you should change your ways.

Now One is All
And All is One.
If you so awaken,
Why worry if you do not win it?

Just believe that your Mind is non-dual
For your Faith in it is not divided.
In it there's no room for word and speech;
It has not present, past or future.

5. *Lu-7*

The smallest is the same as the largest
In the realm where delusion is cut off.
The largest is the same as the smallest;
No boundaries are visible.

Existence is precisely existence.
Emptiness is precisely existence.
If it is not like this,
Then you must not preserve it.

One is everything;
Everything is one.
If you can be like this,
Why worry about not finishing?

Faith and mind are not two;
Non-duality is faith in mind.
The path of words is cut off;
There is no past, no future, no present.

6. *Sheng-yen-7*

7. *Pajin-7*

Very large and small are equal,
The limits cannot be seen.

With being there is nonbeing.
With nonbeing there is being.
If not so
Do not hold on to it.

One is all,
All is one
Merely with such ability
Worry not for finality.

Faith in mind is nondual.
Nonduality is faith in mind.
Discourse here stops
With no past, present, future.

8. *Lombardo-7*

Infinitely large is infinitely small:
Measurements do not matter here.

What is, is the same as what is not.
What is not, is the same as what is.
Where it is not like this,
Do not bother staying.

One is all,
All is one.
When you see things like this,
How can you be incomplete?

Trust and Mind are not two.
Not-two is Trust in Mind.
Here all words stop:
Never were, won't be, aren't now.

Absolute reality is beyond time and space,
Empty and infinite
existing as one,
opening before your eyes,
A vast presence.

The very small and the very large are equal,
boundaries and limits do not exist.

Being and non-being both exist;
for whether you see it or not
is of no consequence.

One thing is all things, and all things are one.
What is and what is not are equals.
Once this is realized
there is no need to worry about anything.

To live and to trust in the non-dual mind
is to move with true freedom,
to live without anxiety,
upon the Great Way.

Language contains no way to describe
the ultimate unity of Suchness:
Beyond belief, beyond expression,
beyond space, beyond time.

9. *Dunn & Jourdan-7*

173

This knowledge is beyond time, long or short,
This knowledge is eternal. It neither is nor is not.

Everywhere is here and the smallest equals the largest.
Space cannot confine anything.
The largest equals the smallest.
There are no boundaries, no within and without.

What is and what is not are the same,
For what is not is equal to what is.

If you do not awaken to this truth,
do not worry yourself about it.

Just believe that your Buddha Mind is not divided,
That it accepts all without judgment.

Give no thoughts to words and speeches or pretty plans
The eternal has no present, past or future.

10. *Hsu Yun-7*

CHINESE TEXT OF THE POEM

(To be read down each column starting on the left.)

信心銘

至道無難	兩處失功	能隨境滅	勿惡六塵	泯其所以	皆入此宗
唯嫌揀擇	遣有沒有	境逐能沈	六塵不惡	不可方比	宗非促延
但莫憎愛	從空背空	境由能境	還同正覺	止動無動	一念萬年
洞然明白	多言多慮	能由境能	智者無爲	動止無止	無在不在
毫釐有差	轉不相應	欲知兩段	愚人自縛	兩既不成	十方目前
天地懸隔	絕言絕慮	元是一空	法無異法	一何有爾	極小同大
欲得現前	無處不通	一空同兩	妄自愛著	究竟窮極	忘絕境界
莫存順逆	歸根得旨	齊含萬象	將心用心	不存軌則	極大同小
違順相爭	隨照失宗	不見精麄	豈非大錯	契心平等	不見邊表
是爲心病	須臾返照	寧有偏黨	迷生寂亂	所作俱息	有即是無
不識玄旨	勝卻前空	大道體寬	悟無好惡	狐疑盡淨	無即是有
徒勞念靜	前空轉變	無易無難	一切二邊	正信調直	若不如此
圓同太虛	皆由妄見	小見狐疑	妄自斟酌	一切不留	必不相守
無欠無餘	不用求眞	轉急轉遲	夢幻虛華	無可記憶	一即一切
良由取捨	唯須息見	執之失度	何勞把捉	虛明自照	一切即一
所以不如	二見不住	必入邪路	得失是非	不勞心力	但能如是
莫逐有緣	慎莫追尋	放之自然	一時放卻	非思量處	何慮不畢
勿住空忍	纔有是非	體無去住	眼若不睡	識情難測	信心不二
一種平懷	紛然失心	任性合道	諸夢自除	眞如法界	不二信心
泯然自盡	二由一有	逍遙絕惱	心若不異	無他無自	言語道斷
止動歸止	一亦莫守	繫念乖眞	萬法一如	要急相應	非去來今
止更彌動	一心不生	昏沈不好	一如體玄	唯言不二	
唯滯兩邊	萬法無咎	不好勞神	兀爾忘虛	不二皆同	
寧知一種	無咎無法	何用疏親	萬法齊觀	無不包容	
一種不通	不生不心	欲取一乘	歸復自然	十方智者	

⊰ Appendix III ⊱

EXCERPTS ON EMPTINESS FROM HEART SUTRA AND
DIAMOND SUTRA COMMENTARIES BY MU SOENG

AS MENTIONED in the introductory section, I have chosen to put the excerpts on shunyata (emptiness) from my commentaries on the Heart Sutra and the Diamond Sutra in the form of an appendix rather than slow down the narrative flow in that section. The term "emptiness" has become such an integral part of any discussion about Buddhist teachings in the contemporary West that a fuller discussion of the term seems warranted if only to set the record straight. Translating the Sanskrit word *shunyata* into Western languages has always been problematic. When translated as "voidness" or "emptiness," it has a nihilistic undertone, which is how the orientalists of the nineteenth century saw and portrayed Buddhism. In their translations of *Xinxinming*, even pioneering scholars like D. T. Suzuki and R. H. Blyth fall into this trap and translate *shunyata* as "the Void." I shudder to think of the confusion it must have caused for a whole generation of Zen readers in the West, given the fact that for a long time Suzuki's were the only translations of Zen texts available to the average reader. The following passages from my commentary on the Diamond Sutra[64] (these also include the comments in my earlier commentary on the Heart Sutra) give the interested reader an extensive background in the use of this term, and how such understanding might in turn have a bearing on unpacking the sentiments in the poem under consideration here.

Fortunately our understanding of the term and of Buddhism itself has grown in recent decades and has prevailed over the earlier misinterpretations. The Buddhist usage of this verb in the compound term "shunyata" is to indicate the true nature of a swelling or a bubble, which appears to be an enclosure but is in reality hollow or contentless. In the Buddhist wisdom tradition, its usage is as a tool to distinguish between appearance and reality. When one is deluded, one operates on the assumption that what is apprehended by the senses (that is, the bubble) contains something identifiable or graspable; the corrective application of prajna-wisdom allows one to see that all appearances are illusory, with nothing inherent to grasp. This prajna-wisdom does not automatically invalidate appearances but challenges us to investigate the nature of reality more closely.

Shunyata (Pali: *sunnata*) is a concept that appears in the Pali Canon but was generally ignored by the Abhidharma systematizers. In the Pali sutras, this term was used in a twofold sense: (1) a direct mode of perception in which nothing is added to or subtracted from the actual data perceived. This modal-ity of perception perceives thought as a thought irrespective of the contents of the thought, without attending to the question of whether or not there is a thinker; when something is apprehended in a visual field, it perceives it to be an experience of seeing rather than affirming or denying the existence of an object behind the experience, and so forth, in each of the sense organs and their function. In this modality nirvana is considered to be the highest form of shunyata in the present life, as the uncorrupted mode of awareness of things as they are; and (2) the lack of a selfhood (anything incapable of self-identification) in the six senses and their objects. In other words, shun-yata was both a mode of perception and an attribute of things perceived.

The Abhidharmists had maintained that even though an individual per-son was empty of self, there were dharmas that had their "own-being" (svabhava) and were the building blocks of the universe. In a certain sense, this theory is akin to the Newtonian particle theory in physics. Early Maha-yana thinkers attacked this notion and accused the Abhidharmists of being attached to a subtle notion of "self" in the dharmas, of being substantialists, and thus unable to truly understand the Buddha's teachings. Their thinking was helped considerably by parallel developments in the science of mathe-matics in India at that time.

In the fourth century BCE., the linguist Panini had developed the concept of zero (Sanskrit, shunya) to symbolize empty but func-tioning positions in his analysis of Sanskrit grammar. (He pro-posed that every word was composed of a root and a suffix, so words without suffixes actually had the zero suffix.) Mathemati-cians eventually borrowed the concept to supply an essential prin-ciple of the decimal notation we use today: that a place in a system may be empty (like the zeros in 10,000) but can still function in relationship to the rest of the system.[65]

The central doctrinal controversy between the Abhidharmists and the early Mahayana thinkers thus rested on the formers' assertion that the irreducible dharmas forming the ultimate building blocks of experience were each endowed with svabhava, their own particular being or nature. The Mahayanists posited that all dharmas were empty of svabhava. Even though conditional relations (between two dharmas) functioned as interdependent co-arising,

> ... there were no "essences" acting as nodes in the relationships, just as mathematical relationships could function among the integers in the decimal notation even if they were only zeroes. In fact, if dharmas had any essence, the principles of causation and the Four Noble Truths could not operate, for essences by nature cannot change, and thus cannot be subject to causal conditions. Whether the Abhidharmists meant the concept of svabhava to imply an unchanging essence is a moot point, but in time the doctrine of emptiness became a rallying point for the rejection of the entire Abhidharma enterprise.[66]

One way to understand the controversy between the Abhidharmists and the early Mahayana thinkers is through the parallel developments in physics between the Newtonian atomic theory, which corresponds to the Abhidharma position, and quantum subatomic theory, which corresponds to the Mahayana position.

In my commentary on the Heart Sutra I have attempted to point out how the findings of quantum physics have added a new dimension to our understanding the meaning of the term shunyata and what it stands for. Here are some excerpts from that commentary as they bear on a discussion of shunyata:

For a very long time, the Newtonian/Cartesian scientific view of the world rested on the notion of solid, indestructible particles as the building blocks of matter and all life, moving in space and influencing each other by forces of gravitation and interacting according to fixed and unchangeable laws. This myth disintegrated under the impact of the experimental and theoretical evidence produced by quantum physicists in the early decades of this century. The experiments of quantum physics showed that the atoms, the presumed fundamental building blocks of the universe, were, at their core, essentially empty. In experiments, subatomic particles showed the same paradoxical

nature as light, manifesting either as particles or waves depending on how the
experiment was set up.

Quantum physics has thus brought about a radical new understanding
both of the particles and the void. In subatomic physics, mass is no longer
seen as a material substance but is recognized as a form of energy. When a
piece of seemingly solid matter—a rock or a human hand or the limb of a
tree—is placed under a powerful electronic microscope:

> The electron-scanning microscope, with the power to magnify
> several thousand times, takes us down into a realm that has the
> look of the sea about it. In the kingdom of the corpuscles, there is
> transfiguration and there is samsara, the endless round of birth
> and death. Every passing second, some 2–1/2 million red cells are
> born; every second, the same number die. The typical cell lives
> about 110 days, then becomes tired and decrepit. There are no lin-
> gering deaths here, for when a cell loses its vital force, it somehow
> attracts the attention of macrophage.
>
> As the magnification increases, the flesh does begin to dissolve.
> Muscle fiber now takes on a fully crystalline aspect. We can see
> that it is made of long, spiral molecules in orderly array. And all of
> these molecules are swaying like wheat in the wind, connected
> with one another and held in place by invisible waves that pulse
> many trillions of times a second.
>
> What are the molecules made of? As we move closer, we see
> atoms, the tiny shadowy balls dancing around their fixed locations
> in the molecules, sometimes changing position with their part-
> ners in perfect rhythms. And now we focus on one of the atoms;
> its interior is lightly veiled by a cloud of electrons. We come closer,
> increasing the magnification. The shell dissolves and we look on
> the inside to find . . . nothing.
>
> Somewhere within that emptiness, we know is a nucleus. We
> scan the space, and there it is, a tiny dot. At last, we have discov-
> ered something hard and solid, a reference point. But no! As we
> move closer to the nucleus, it too begins to dissolve. It too is noth-
> ing more than an oscillating field, waves of rhythm. Inside the
> nucleus are other organized fields: protons, neutrons, even smaller

"particles." Each of these, upon our approach, also dissolve into pure rhythm.

These days they (the scientists) are looking for quarks, strange subatomic entities, having qualities which they describe with such words as upness, downness, charm, strangeness, truth, beauty, color, and flavor. But no matter. If we could get close enough to these wondrous quarks, they too would melt away. They too would have to give up all pretense of solidity. Even their speed and relationship would be unclear, leaving them only relationship and pattern of vibration.

Of what is the body made? It is made of emptiness and rhythm. At the ultimate heart of the body, at the heart of the world, there is no solidity. Once again, there is only the dance.

(At) the unimaginable heart of the atom, the compact nucleus, we have found no solid object, but rather a dynamic pattern of tightly confined energy vibrating perhaps 1022 times a second: a dance. The protons—the positively charged knots in the pattern of the nucleus—are not only powerful; they are very old. Along with the much lighter electrons that spin and vibrate around the outer regions of the atom, the protons constitute the most ancient entities of matter in the universe, going back to the first seconds after the birth of space and time.[67]

It follows then that in the world of subatomic physics there are no objects, only processes. Atoms consist of particles and these particles are not made of any solid material substance. When we observe them under a microscope, we never see any substance; we rather observe dynamic patterns, continually changing into one another—a continuous dance of energy. This dance of energy, the underlying rhythm of the universe, is again more intuited than seen. Jack Kornfield, a contemporary teacher of meditation, finds a parallel between the behavior of subatomic particles and meditational states:

When the mind becomes very silent, you can clearly see that all that exists in the world are brief moments of consciousness arising together with the six sense objects. There is only sight and the knowing of sight, sound and the knowing of sound, smell, taste and the knowing of them, thoughts and the knowing of thoughts. If you can make the mind very focused, as you can in meditation, you see that the whole breaks down into these small events of sight and the knowing, sound and the knowing and thought and the knowing. No longer are these houses, cars, bodies, or even oneself. All you see are particles of consciousness as experience. Yet you can go deep in meditation in another way and the mind becomes very still. You will see differently that consciousness is like waves, like a sea, an ocean. Now it is not particles but instead every sight and sound is contained in this ocean of consciousness. From this perspective, there is no sense of particles at all.[68]

Energy, whether of wave or particle, is associated with activity, with dynamic change. Thus the core of the universe—whether we see it as the heart of the atom or our own consciousness—is not static but a state of constant and dynamic change. This energy—now wave, now particle—infuses each and every form at the cellular level. No form exists without being infused by this universal energy; form and energy interpenetrate each other endlessly in an ever-changing dance of the molecules, creating our universe. This universal energy is itself a process, beyond the confines of time and space; a form, on the other hand, is an "event," existing momentarily in time and space. This "moment" may last for seventy or eighty years in the case of a human being, a thousand years in the case of a sequoia tree, a few million years in the case of a mountain, but internally, at the cellular level, each of these forms is in a process of change at any given moment. In the paradigms of quantum physics, there is ceaseless change at the core of the universe; in the paradigm of Mahayana wisdom, there too is ceaseless change at the core of our consciousness and of the universe.

The new paradigm in quantum physics is a replacement of atomism/reductionism with dynamic qualities of web relationships. It a replacement of the Cartesian/Newtonian formulation of an objective world "out there" that can be investigated independently of the investigator, with an interconnected "ecological" model in which the investigator is not separated from the object of investigation and whose "being" affects the quality of investigation as much as the object itself. This paradigm of quantum physics parallels the Mahayana wisdom (prajnaparamita) of ancient India that sees each and every form as a compounded entity, created and held in place, quite momentarily, by a number of conditioning factors coming together. Because it is a compounded entity, it has no core independent of the conditioning factors that are responsible for its creation. Hence it is empty of a core, an own-being (svabhava) or self-essence (svabhavata); it is rather made up of a web of relationships that are dynamic in character and are interconnected in complex ways in which the observer and the observed share equally the responsibility for the momentary appearance of phenomena.

David Bohm, one of the leading physicists of this century, sees the tangible reality of our everyday lives as a kind of illusion—like a holographic image. In his work, Bohm postulates two orders of reality: the surfacial is the "explicate" or the "unfolded" order while the deeper level is the "implicate" or the "enfolded" order. The universe is a result of countless "enfoldings" and "unfoldings" between these two orders:

> Electrons and all other particles are no more substantive or permanent than the form a geyser of water takes as it gushes out of a fountain. They are sustained by the constant flux from the implicate order, and when a particle appears to be destroyed, it is not lost. It has merely enfolded back into the deeper order from which it sprang.
>
> The constant and flowing exchange between the two orders explains how particles, such as the electron in the postironium atom, can shapeshift from one kind of particle to another. Such shiftings can be viewed as one particle, say an electron, enfolding back into the implicate order while another, a photon, unfolds and takes its place. It also explains how a quantum can manifest as either a particle or a wave.[69]

In a model paralleling the geyser of water gushing out of the fountain, the later Mahayana-Yogachara teachings posit that the five skandhas (conglomerations—of materiality, feelings, perceptions, mental formations, and consciousness) are constantly arising out of shunyata or Dharmakaya (literally, the body of truth).

The Yogachara formulations in later Mahayana sought to "improve" the purely dialectical approach of the earlier Madhyamika in an understanding of shunyata. In this Yogachara formulation, shunyata is equated with Dharmakaya and used in the sense of "ground of being," or the Implicate Order in quantum physics proposed by David Bohm. When each of the skandhas has run its course, it merely enfolds back into shunyata. In their transitory and momentary appearance they are constantly interacting with one another and each interaction produces a bija (seed or imprint). This imprint is what enfolds back into shunyata or Dharmakaya. In Yogachara, both shunyata and Dharmakaya are synonymous with Tathagatagarbha, the "womb of the Tathagata" which stands for a cosmic consciousness as a container of individual and collective karmic seeds but which in itself remains unstained by such seeds.

Naturally, Bohm does not address the issue of any imprints resulting from the mutual interactions of the implicate and the explicate orders which is the domain of Buddhist perspectives on karma and rebirth. In Yogachara formulations of alaya-vijnana, the "store-house consciousness," there is the notion of "seeds" resulting from an encounter of the six senses with the phenomenal world, falling into the store-consciousness which is akin to our subconscious mind. How these seeds interact with "old" seeds already present in the store-consciousness and "new" seeds that might be coming in even as a particular seed is finding its "locality" in the store-consciousness is a matter of great psychological interest and research. There is indeed a great deal of interest currently in the psychological understandings of the Buddhist tradition, and both traditions are all the richer for it.

The Bohmian interplay of the implicate and the explicate orders can be seen by Buddhist thinkers as the interplay of the absolute and the relative. At the implicate level, there is an incredible amount of energy that is the same energy that produces streaking comets, burning stars, and scattering radiation in the cosmos; the explicate order is a manifestation of that energy but it collapses back into the underlying implicate order. The energy at the implicate level is absolute for it is indivisible; its manifestation in the world of forms (as in a geyser) is the realm of the relative, and the absolute and the relative are in a dynamic interdependent relationship. Theoretically, the absolute need not be in an interdependent relationship but in our experience as human beings we do not encounter the absolute as a stand-alone absolute; we encounter it through the relative.

In order to protect us from utter despair (if we were to get fixated on the notion of absolute as a stand-alone entity), the Madhyamika thinkers in early Mahayana had advanced the "Two Truths Theory." The Two-Truths theory helped Mahayana thinkers bridge the apparent incompatibility between emptiness and compassion by accepting the relative, qualified truth of the realm of appearances. Nirvana and samsara are seen as conflation or synergetic loops as in the Bohmian model. Thus the relative truth of the experience of dukkha (unsatisfactoriness) could be accepted and a compassionate perspective brought to it without compromising the ultimate or absolute truth of emptiness. In the best sense of the term, the Yogacharins saw their own formulation as another Upaya rather than as an ideology to be defended.

Modern physics sees the speed of light as the absolute; what is relative is time and space. The absolute and mysterious nature of the speed of light forms a bridge from the relative, objective world we see around us to the infinite realm beyond time-space. Physicists now describe all matter as frozen light. Paradoxically, this frozen light is also a dynamic movement and the cause of incalculable enfoldings and unfoldings between the two orders.

> The existence of a deeper and holographically organized order also explains why reality becomes nonlocal at the subquantum level. Because everything in the cosmos is made out of the seamless holographic fabric of the implicate order, it is as meaningless to view the universe as composed of parts, as it is to view the different geysers in a fountain as separate from the water out of which they flow. Despite the apparent separability of things at the explicate level, everything is a seamless extension of everything else, and ultimately even the implicate and the explicate orders blend into each other.[70]

While quantum physics sees the two orders as energy configurations blending into each other—and ultimately inseparable—so did the Mahayana thinkers see the mutual identity and inseparability of samsara and nirvana—"Form does not differ from emptiness, emptiness does not differ from form"—as a way of being in the world, being free from rigid ideologies, and willing to help all beings in the process of liberation. This is the path of the bodhisattva on the way to Buddhahood.

This detailed discussion of shunyata hopefully provides a basic frame of reference for the "Oneness" of which the poem *Trust in Mind* speaks so often.

Part of the problem in early Buddhist philosophical tradition was that the Buddha had not spoken of any kind of a substratum. Apart from one single reference to the "unconditioned," there is no positive mention of a substratum in the Pali sutras. The radical deconstruction of the Buddha was a huge jump for the ordinary human mind to integrate. The Madhyamika dialectic was not very helpful in bridging this gap either. While this deconstruction may have been fine for scholar-monks to work with, it gave rise to a number of internal pressures that in turn became the basic building blocks of the Mahayana movement in India. I have discussed these developments at some length in my commentary on the Diamond Sutra.

At different stages of Mahayana doctrinal developments, various names have been used for shunyata, such as the Absolute, Tathagatagarbha, Buddha Mind, Buddha Nature, Dharmakaya, Dharmadhatu, Pure Mind, True Self, Pure Being, and so on, depending on the particular sub-tradition and its own internal development. Hopefully, in the best sense of the usage, each one of these terms is talking about the nondual state, the mind that does not make any discrimination.

In early Chan, Tao and One Mind became synonymous with shunyata. These two terms along with Buddha-Mind, Buddha-Nature, and Dharmakaya provide the core vocabulary of the Chan tradition. Sengcan uses the term One Mind in a consistent manner is and its doctrinal understanding, as we have seen, are embedded in the shunyata paradigm. It is instructive that when shunyata is translated into European languages as "Emptiness" or "Voidness" the feeling-tone of the term changes dramatically. A negative value system is implied in such usage. For Sengcan, One Mind is shunyata positively stated.

⋘ Notes ⋙

1. Hu Shih, "Development of Zen Buddhism in China" in *Anthology of Zen* (edited by William A. Briggs), p. 13.

2. Grigg, *The Tao of Zen*, p. xiii.

3. Sheng-yen, *The Poetry of Enlightenment*, p. 2.

4. Dumoulin, *Zen Enlightenment*, p. 28.

5. Conze, *A Short History of Buddhism*, p. 16.

6. Merton, *Mystics and Zen Masters*, p. ix.

7. Waltham, *Chuang Tzu: Genius of the Absurd*, pp. 22–23.

8. Sheng-yen, *Faith in Mind*, p. 2.

9. Bhikkhu Bodhi, "Uniqueness of the Buddha's Doctrine," Buddhist Publications Society Newsletter, No. 48, 2001.

10. Bhikkhu Nanamoli (tr.), *Visuddhimagga*, IX, 96.

11. Rahula, Yogavacara, "The Role of Equanimity: Balancing Effort and Understanding" in *The Bhavana Magazine*, Vol. 5 No. 1, Spring 2003, p. 3.

12. Batchelor, *Verses from the Center*, various, pp. 9–23.

13. Masao,Abe. *Kenosis and Emptiness* in *Buddhist Emptiness and Christian Trinity* (eds. Roger Corless and Paul F. Knitter), p. 20.

14. Ibid., pp. 20–21.

15. Ibid., p. 22.

16. Wright, *Studies in Chinese Buddhism*, p. 2, also p. 125 fn.

17. Waltham, *Chuang Tzu*, p. 17.

18. Ibid., p. 18.

19. Hoover, *The Zen Experience*, p. 8.

20. Waltham, *Chuang Tzu*, p. 19.

21. Ibid., pp. 20–21.

22. Chen, *Buddhism in China*, p. 17.

23. Wright, *Studies in Chinese Buddhism*, p. 8.

24. Watts, *Tao: The Watercourse Way*, p. 76.

25. Zaehner, *Concordant Discord*, pp. 214–15.

26. Chen, *Buddhism in China*, p. 61.

27. Waltham, *Chuang Tzu*, p. 18.

28. Blyth, *Zen and Zen Classics*, vol. 1, p. 50.

29. Hoover, *Zen Experience*, p.14, quoted from Liebenthal.

30. Ibid., p. 14, quoted from Liebenthal.

31. Dumoulin, *A History of Zen Buddhism*, vol. 1, p. 60.

32. Hu Shih, in Briggs, p. 14.

33. Hoover, *Zen Experience*, p. 15.

34. Yampolsky (tr.), *The Platform Sutra of the Sixth Patriarch*, p. 137.

35. Paul, *Philosophy of Mind in Sixth-Century China*, p. 3.

36. Ibid., p. 4.

37. Dumoulin, *A History of Zen Buddhism* Vol.1, p. 76

38. Soeng, *Diamond Sutra*, p. 35.

39. Ibid., pp. 37–38.

40. Ibid., p. 38.

41. Conze, *Short History of Buddhism*, p. 50.

42. Stanley Lombardo. Private communication, September 2003.

43. Sheng-yen, *The Poetry of Enlightenment*, p. 23.

44. Hershock, *Liberating Intimacy*, p. 67.

45. Kornfield and Breiter (eds.) *A Still Forest Pool*, frontispiece.

46. Walker, *Hua Hu Ching*, p. 5.

47. Watts, *The Watercourse Way*, pp. 89–90.

48. Soma Thera, *Kalama Sutta*, p. 5.

49. Quoted in Loy, *Nonduality*, p. 97.

50. Garfield, *The Fundamental Wisdom of the Middle Way*, p. 212.

51. Hershock, *Liberating Intimacy*, p. 68.

52. Ajahn Chah, (see quote # 45 on page above).

53. Wilber, *One Taste*, pp. 27–28.

54. Ibid., p. 26.

55. Ibid., p. 30.

56. Collinson et al., "Zhuangzi" in *Fifty Eastern Thinkers*, pp. 250–51.

57. Seung Sahn, *Compass of Zen*, private printing at Providence Zen Center.

58. Uchiyama, *Opening the Hand of Thought*, p. 160.

59. Nyanaponika Thera and Bhikkhu Bodhi, *Anguttara Nikaya: The Numerical Discourses of the Buddha*, p. 36.

60. Stryk and Ikemoto, *Zen Poems of China and Japan*, p. xlvi.

61. T. S. Eliot, "Burnt Norton," *Collected Poems 1909–1962*, p. 175.

62. Waley, *Three Ways of Thought in Ancient China*, pp. 8–9.

63. Nanamoli, *The Middle Length Discourses of the Buddha*, p. 1039.

64. Soeng, *The Diamond Sutra*, pp. 41–49.

65. Ibid., p. 42, quoted from Robinson, *The Buddhist Religion*.

66. Ibid., p. 42, quoted from Robinson, *The Buddhist Religion*.

67. Ibid,. p. 45, quoted from Leonard, *The Silent Pulse*.

68. Ibid., p. 45, quote from Kornfield, *The Smile of the Buddha: Paradigms in Perspective*.

69. Ibid., p. 47, quoted from Talbot, *The Holographic Universe*.

70. Ibid., p. 49, quoted from Talbot, *The Holographic Universe*.

⊰ Bibliography ⊱

Batchelor, Stephen. *Verses from the Center: A Buddhist Vision of the Sublime*. New York: Riverhead Books, 2000.

Blofeld, John. *The Zen Teaching of Huang Po*. New York: Grove Press, 1958.

Blyth, R. H. *Zen and Zen Classics, Vol. 1*. Tokyo: The Hokuseido Press, 1960.

Briggs, William A. (ed.), *Anthology of Zen*. New York: Grove Press, 1961.

Buswell, Robert. *The Collected Works of Chinul*. Honolulu: University of Hawaii Press, 1983.

Chen, Kenneth. *Buddhism in China: A Historical Survey*. Princeton: Princeton University Press, 1964.

Clarke, Richard. *Hsin Hsin Ming: Verses on the Faith-Mind*. Buffalo, NY: White Pine Press, 1973, 1984.

Collinson, Diane, K. Plant, and R. Wilkinson (eds.). *Fifty Eastern Thinkers*. London: Routledge, 2000.

Conze, Edward. *A Short History of Buddhism*. London: Unwin Paperbacks, 1982.

Corless, Roger, and Paul F. Knitter (eds.) *Buddhist Emptiness and Christian Trinity*. New York: Paulist Press, 1990.

Creel, Herlee G. *What is Taoism? And Other Studies in Chinese Cultural History*. Chicago: University of Chicago Press, 1970.

Dumoulin, Heinrich. *Zen Enlightenment: Origins and Meaning*. New York: Weatherhill, 1979.

———*A History of Zen Buddhism*. London: Faber & Faber, 1959.

Dunn, Philip, and Peter Jourdan (trans.) *The Book of Nothing*. Kansas City: Andrews McMeel Publishing, 2002.

Eliot, T. S. *Collected Poems 1909-1962*. New York: Harcourt, Brace and World, 1963.

Garfield, Jay. *The Fundamental Wisdom of the Middle Way*. New York: Oxford University Press, 1995.

Grigg, Ray. *The Tao of Zen*. Boston: Charles E. Tuttle Co., 1994.

Gyato, Lobsang. *The Harmony of Emptiness and Dependent-Arising*. Dharamsala, India: Library of Tibetan Works and Archives, 1992.

Hershock, Peter D. *Liberating Intimacy: Enlightenment and Social Virtuosity in Chan Bud-dhism*. Albany: State University of New York Press, 1996.

Hoover, Thomas. *The Zen Experience*. New York: New American Library, 1980.

Kornfield, Jack. "The Smile of the Buddha: Paradigms in Perspective" in *Ancient Wis-dom and Modern Science*, edited by Stanislav Graf. Albany, NY: State University of New York Press, 1984.

Kornfield, Jack, and Paul Breiter (eds). *A Still Forest Pool: Teachings of Achan Chah*. Wheaton, IL: Quest Books, 1985.

Leonard, George. *The Silent Pulse*. New York: E. P. Dutton, 1978.

Loy, David. *Nonduality: A Study in Comparative Philosophy*. Amherst, NY: Humanity Books, 1998.

Lu, Kuan Yu. *Practical Buddhism*. London: Rider & Co. 1971.

Merton, Thomas. *Mystics and Zen Masters*. New York: Dell Publishing Co., 1961.

Merzel, Dennis Genpo. *The Eye Never Sleeps*. Boston: Shambhala, 1991.

Nanamoli Bhikhhu (tr.). *Visudhimagga: The Path of Purification*. Kandy, Sri Lanka: Bud-dhist Publications Society, 1975.

Nanamoli, Bhikkhu, and Bhikkhu Bodhi (tr.). *The Middle Length Discourses of the Buddha*. Boston: Wisdom Publications, 1995.

Nyanaponika, Thera & Bhikkhu Bodhi (tr.). *Numerical Discourses of the Buddha: An Anthology of the Suttas from the Anguttara Nikaya*. Walnut Creek, CA: AltaMira Press, 1999.

Pajin, Dusan. "On Faith in Mind," *Journal of Oriental Studies*, vol. XXVI, no. 2. Hong Kong, 1988.

Paul, Diana. *The Philosophy of Mind in Sixth-Century China: Paramartha's "Evolution of Consciousness."* Stanford, CA: Stanford University Press, 1984.

Reps, Paul. *Zen Flesh, Zen Bones*. Boston: Charles E. Tuttle Co., 1957.

Robinson, Richard, et al. *The Buddhist Religion*, 4th ed. Belmont, CA: Wadsworth Pub-lishing, 1997.

Sheng-yen, Ven. *Faith in Mind: A Guide to Chan Practice*. Elmhurst, NY: Dharma Drum Publications, 1987.

———The *Poetry of Enlightenment: Poems by Ancient Chan Masters*. Elmhurst, NY: Dharma Drum Publications, 1987.

Soeng, Mu. *Diamond Sutra: Transforming the Way We Perceive the World*. Boston: Wis-dom Publications, 2000.

Sokei-An. *Cat's Yawn*. New York: The First Zen Institute of America, 1947.

Soma, Thera. *Kalama Sutta: Buddha's Charter of Free Inquiry*. Kandy, Sri Lanka: Buddhist Publications Society, Wheel #8, 1981.

Stryk, Lucien, and Takashi Ikemoto. *Zen Poems of China and Japan*. New York: Grove Press, 1973.

Suzuki, D. T. *Essays in Zen Buddhism, First Series*. York Beach, Maine: Samuel Weiser, 1949.

Talbot, Michael. *The Holographic Universe*. New York: HarperCollins, 1991.

Uchiyama, Kosho. *Opening the Hand of Thought*. New York: Arkana/Penguin, 1993.

Waley, Arthur (ed.). *Buddhist Texts Through the Ages*. New York: Harper & Row, 1964.

———*Three Ways of Thought in Ancient China*. New York: Doubleday & Co. (n.d.)

Walker, Brian (tr.). *Hua Hu Ching: The Unknown Teachings of Lao Tzu*. New York: HarperSanFrancisco, 1994.

Waltham, Clae. *Chuang Tzu: Genius of the Absurd*. New York: Ace Books, 1971,

Watts, Alan. *Tao: The Watercourse Way*. New York: Pantheon Books, 1975.

Wilber, Ken. *One Taste*. Shambhala Publications, 2000.

Williams, Paul. *Mahayana Buddhism*. London: Routledge, 1989.

Wright, Arthur F. *Studies in Chinese Buddhism* (Robert M. Somers, ed.). New Haven: Yale University Press, 1990.

Wu, John. *The Golden Age of Zen*. New York: Doubleday, 1967, 1996.

Wu, Yi. *The Mind of Chinese Chan (Zen)*. San Francisco: Great Learning Publishing Co., 1989.

Yampolsky, Philip. *The Platform Sutra of the Sixth Patriarch*. New York: Columbia University Press, 1967.

Zaehner, R. C. *Concordant Discord: The Interdependence of Faiths*. Oxford: Clarendon Press, 1970.

❊ Index ❊

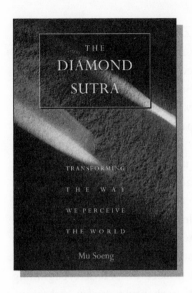

The Diamond Sutra
*Transforming the Way We
Perceive the World*
Mu Soeng
192 pages, ISBN 0-86171-160-2, $16.95

"Mu Soeng's commentary on The Diamond Sutra is a combination of Buddhist history lesson, philosophical investigation, and thorough contemporary reading of this core Mahayana text. He applies both scholarship and years of dharma training to his analysis. A fresh and inspiring exposition of core Mahayana philosophy."—*Inquiring Mind*

Novice to Master
*An Ongoing Lesson in the Extent of
My Own Stupidity*
Soko Morinaga Roshi
Translated by Belenda Attaway Yamakawa
168 pages, ISBN 0-86171-393-1, $11.95

"Anyone who reads this charming memoir can only wish they had the opportunity to meet this modest yet wise man. It provides rich insight into the protocol of training for the life of a Zen abbot, but is, in many ways, universal—a headstrong young man is forced to conform to a wiser force and shed his arrogance to achieve a higher state of knowledge and serenity. *Novice to Master* serves up the most subtle form of enlightenment."—*New York Resident*

On Zen Practice
Body, Breath, and Mind
Edited by Taizan Maezumi Roshi
and Bernie Glassman
Foreword by Robert Aitken
208 pages, ISBN 0-86171-315-x, $16.95

This updated landmark volume makes available for the first time in decades the teachings that were formative to a whole generation of American Zen teachers and students. Conceived as the essential Zen primer, *OZP* addresses every aspect of practice: beginning practice, chanting, *sesshin*, *shikantaza*, working with Mu, the nature of koans, and more.

On Zen Practice's contributors are regarded as some of modern Zen's foremost teachers, and are largely responsible for Zen's steady growth in America. This newly refined volume is an unmatched teaching and reference tool for today's Zen practitioner.

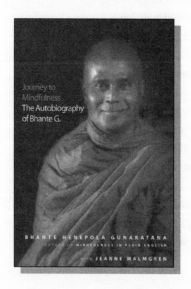

Journey to Mindfulness
The Autobiography of Bhante G.
Bhante Henepola Gunaratana
240 pages, ISBN 0-86171-347-8, $16.95

"Bhante Gunaratana's stature across America as a Buddhist teacher has risen with the popularity of his classic *Mindfulness in Plain English*. While Bhante's narrative doesn't leave out the hard parts, this is still, of course, a success story. And here lies the promise and purpose of *Journey to Mindfulness*: if Bhante G. can do it, so can you."
—*Shambhala Sun*

Mindfulness Yoga
The Awakened Union of Breath,
Body, and Mind
Frank Jude Boccio
Foreword by Georg Feuerstein
320 pages, 100 photos,
ISBN 0-86171-335-4, $19.95

"I highly recommend this book. Boccio's exposition of the basic principles of mindfulness yoga is elegant, lucid, astonishingly comprehensive, and thoroughly accessible. And the sections on practice are designed—refreshingly—for real human beings! There is something here for everyone, from beginning students to more advanced practitioners alike. Bravo!"
—Stephen Cope, psychotherapist, senior Kripalu Yoga teacher, and author of *Yoga and the Quest for the True Self*

Eihei Dogen
Mystical Realist
Hee-Jin Kim
Foreword by Taigen Dan Leighton
320 pages, ISBN 0-86171-376-1, $19.95

"A beacon of scholarship into the mind of one of the most remarkable spiritual giants in the history of Zen."
—John Daido Loori, abbot of Zen Mountain Monastery

How to Raise an Ox
Zen Practice as Taught in Master Dogen's Shobogenzo
Francis Dojun Cook
Foreword by Taizan Maezumi
208 pages, ISBN 0-86171-317-6, $14.95

"An outstanding introduction to the most important Zen master in Japanese history. Cook has a remarkable grasp of the heart of Dogen's thinking and a genius for communicating it."
—Jeremy D. Safran, Ph.D., editor of *Psychoanalysis and Buddhism: An Unfolding Dialogue*

The Art of Just Sitting
Writings on the Zen Practice of Shikantaza, 2nd Edition
Edited by John Daido Loori
256 pages, ISBN 0-86171-394-X, $16.95

This unparalleled volume offers essential guidance—from the most influential Buddhist masters, and from many of modern Zen's preeminent teachers—on one of Zen's two most central practices. This new edition contains three new translations by renowned scholar-practitioners.

≼ About Wisdom ≽

Wisdom Publications, a not-for-profit publisher, is dedicated to making available authentic Buddhist works for the benefit of all. We publish translations of the sutras and tantras, commentaries and teachings of past and contemporary Buddhist masters, and original works by the world's leading Buddhist scholars. We publish our titles with the appreciation of Buddhism as a living philosophy and with the special commitment to preserve and transmit important works from all the major Buddhist traditions.

To learn more about Wisdom, or to browse books online, visit our website at wisdompubs.org.

You may request a copy of our mail-order catalog online or by writing to:

Wisdom Publications
199 Elm Street
Somerville, Massachusetts 02144 USA
Telephone: (617) 776-7416
Fax: (617) 776-7841
Email: info@wisdompubs.org
www.wisdompubs.org

THE WISDOM TRUST

As a not-for-profit publisher, Wisdom is dedicated to the publication of fine Dharma books for the benefit of all sentient beings and dependent upon the kindness and generosity of sponsors in order to do so. If you would like to make a donation to Wisdom, please do so through our Somerville office. If you would like to sponsor the publication of a book, please write or email us at the address above.

Thank you.

Wisdom is a nonprofit, charitable 501(c)(3) organization affiliated with the Foundation for the Preservation of the Mahayana Tradition (FPMT).